EAST

of

THORNTON

JUNCTION

The Story of the FifeCoast Line

James K. Corstorphine

*A short history of the
Railway line from
Thornton to Leuchars
which ran around the
East Neuk of Fife*

Published by:

**Wast-By Books
26 Friday Walk
Lower Largo
Fife
Scotland
KY8 6FB**

First Published in 1995

Revised and adapted for electronic publication in 2013

This edition © 2018 James K. Corstorphine
(ISBN 9781976909283)

By the Same Author:

The Earliest Fife Football Clubs
(ISBN 9781980249580)

Our Boys and the Wise Men: The Origins of Dundee Football Club
(ISBN 9798643521549)

On That Windswept Plain: the First 100 Years of East Fife F.C.
(ISBN 9781976888618)

Peter Smith, the Fisherman Poet of Cellardyke
(ISBN 9798644727827)

All of the above titles are available in both paperback and Kindle eBook format from: Amazon.co.uk

Introduction

*A **Thomson Class B1** passes the **WaidAcademy** as it approaches Anstruther station from the east in the 1960's (Author's Collection).*

One of my earliest memories is that of standing on the platform at Anstruther railway station on a sunny Saturday morning at the age of five, waiting for the train to take our family to Edinburgh for a day out. This was not an infrequent experience, as even at that early age I was accustomed to boarding the green 'Diesel Multiple Units' at Anstruther to go here and there on outings with older members of the family.

I was pleasantly surprised on this occasion, however, to see a big dirty black steam engine, which by this time was becoming something of a rarity on Britain's railways, pass under the road bridge beside the Waid Academy and come to a stop beside us. After being lifted over the gap between the platform and the maroon coaches, I sat down in a compartment of what was my first experience of a corridor train.

For most of the journey I occupied myself by reading a comic that had been bought for me at the station bookstall, occasionally glancing out of the carriage window as the train passed through the villages and stations dotted along the Fife coast. I can vividly remember gazing out of the window on this particular journey as the train passed through a large railway yard full of steam engines that were due to be scrapped, according to a smartly dressed gentleman in the same compartment. Steam trains, he explained to me, would soon be a thing of the past.

Sadly, both steam and diesel trains in the east of Fife are now only a memory, but it is this memory that prompted me to do some research into the history of the Fife Coast Line, which has resulted in the publication of this book. The Fife Coast Line was the name lovingly bestowed on that part of the British Rail network that stretched from Thornton around the coast to Leuchars and was constructed in six stages by four separate companies during a thirty five year period from 1851 to 1887.

The first section to be opened was the Leuchars to St Andrews railway in 1852, closely followed by the Thornton to Leven railway in 1854. The line between Leven and Anstruther was built in two stages; the first stage between Leven and Kilconquhar being opened in 1857, with Anstruther being reached six years later in 1863. The railway connecting Anstruther with St Andrews was also built in two stages. In 1883 the line was opened between Anstruther and Boarhills, but it was to be another four years before the last section between Boarhills and St Andrews was completed in 1887.

The first part of the line to close to passengers was the St Andrews to Leven section. Although I cannot claim to have been on the last train on that particular section, which left Crail bound for Glasgow on Sunday 5th September 1965, I did have the "pleasure" of being on the last train to travel in the opposite direction between Anstruther and Crail earlier that evening.

The lines from Thornton to Leven and from Leuchars to St Andrews were both closed to passengers in 1969, although the Leven area remained connected to the rail network on a goods only basis for many years after this.

This book covers the history of the Fife Coast Line, from the first sod being cut in 1851 to the final section being closed to passengers in 1969 and includes a brief look at the section of the railway which remained open until the early 21st century to serve Methil Power Station, Methil Docks and Cameron Bridge Distillery; as well as considering the possibility of passenger services being re-introduced over certain parts of the line.

Hopefully the book will not only be of interest to railway enthusiasts, but to everyone who remembers railways in Fife prior to the Beeching cuts of the 1960's.

Footnote: When referring to the Fife coastal village of St Monans in this book, I have used the now out of date method of spelling the village's name. The reason for this is simply that throughout the entire history of the FifeCoast Line, the village was officially known as St Monance.

Contents

Chapter One

THE NEED FOR A RAILWAY

STEAM
TO
EDINBURGH, GLASGOW, & the SOUTH.

The Edinburgh and Dundee Steam-
Packet Company's New Steam-
Ship
"BRITANNIA,"
SAILS REGULARLY
FROM DUNDEE FOR GRANTON PIER
Every afternoon at Two o'clock;
AND FROM GRANTON PIER
Every morning at Eight o'clock;—
Making the Passage in Four Hours—
CALLING AT ELIE, ANSTRUTHER, AND CRAIL.
FARES:—
Cabin, 4s.; Steerage, 2s. 6d.

₊ Parties from Edinburgh, returning same day,
one Fare only; and Pleasure Parties on Saturdays,
from Dundee, returning on Mondays, one Fare only.

This fine new Iron Steamer BRITANNIA, of 207 Tons
Register and 150 Horse Power, of a beautiful model
by Mr W. Denny, is fitted up in a commodious style,
with separate State Rooms for parties or families,
water-tight Bulkheads, Life-Boats on deck, and other
improvements; and will materially abridge the time
hitherto taken on this passage.

Mr Croall's Coaches leave the Duty-House, Edinburgh; and Mr Coulston's Coach leaves his Office,
Leith, at half-past Seven morning, and wait the ves-
sel's arrival.

FROM EDINBURGH—The BRITANNIA will arrive in
time for the Evening Train to Glasgow at half-past
Seven.
FROM GRANTON—Steamer to Berwick and Newcastle
every Tuesday, Wednesday, and Friday morning at
Seven o'clock, and every Saturday afternoon at Six
o'clock—FARES, 10s. and 6s.
FROM LEITH—Steamer to Hull every Wednesday and
Saturday, about High Water—FARES, 12s. and 7s.
6d.
JOHN BELL, AGENT.
Dundee, September 1845.

Advertisements for sea travel to and from the East Neuk of Fife
appeared in most newspapers during the early to mid 1800's

1840 heralded the dawn of the railway age in the Fife
peninsula when the Edinburgh and Northern Railway
Company proposed the first railway line in Fife. By the time
this line opened from Burntisland to Cupar in 1847, many
branch lines diverging from this main line had been proposed
by smaller independent railway companies seeking to bring
prosperity to the more remote corners of the county. The

1

reasons for this are made clear when we consider how isolated some of the small village communities were at this time and the difficulties encountered when travelling to and from these places by land or sea.

In the 1840's, two steamships sailed between Edinburgh and Largo every day, carrying on average no fewer than 220 passengers. Connection with the towns and villages of Anstruther, Elie, St. Andrews and Ceres with the ship at Largo was by stagecoach. Ships plying between the ports of Granton and Dundee also called at the East Neuk ports of Anstruther, Pittenweem and Elie twice daily, with ships from Montrose and Aberdeen calling less frequently.

The dangers of sea travel during the middle of the nineteenth century are well documented in the newspapers of the 1840's, with reports of mishaps at sea being commonplace. One such occurrence reported in the "Fifeshire Journal" at this time tells of a passenger ship sailing between Edinburgh and Leven in thick fog losing her way and "happening upon the port of Largo" by chance!

Another option open to travellers between Fife and Edinburgh during the 1840's was a stagecoach which travelled twice daily from Anstruther along the coast to Burntisland and then crossed the Forth by ferry to Granton. One can only imagine the long and tedious journey endured by passengers using this mode of transport.

Of these early years, 1845 was undoubtedly the year that 'Railway mania' took hold of Fife, with no fewer than sixteen railway schemes being proposed, some being more ambitious than others. One such scheme proposed a railway running south from Cupar to Largo by way of Dura Den, necessitating the construction of a tunnel under Largo Law!

Another proposal was to construct a railway to Elie harbour, from where a steam ferry service would be established to North Berwick. A railway would then be constructed from

North Berwick to connect with the main line south to England. The promoters of this railway considered their proposals to be a serious alternative to the Burntisland to Granton ferry service, providing a fast route from north eastern Scotland to London and the English markets.

It was in September of 1845 that the prospectus for the first East of Fife Railway Company was published. The promoters of this company were mainly local businessmen and dignitaries, whose principle aim was to connect the East Neuk of Fife with the rest of the country. In the words of the prospectus, the company was formed with the view of:

"extending the benefits of railway communication to the district lying on the South and Eastern coast of Fife, from the Edinburgh and Northern Railway to the Burgh of Anstruther"

The line was to be twenty miles long, branching from the Edinburgh and Northern railway at Thornton or Markinch and then heading eastwards either along the valley of the River Ore or the River Leven as appropriate. The railway would then pass by or near to CameronBridge distillery and the villages and hamlets of Kennoway, Leven, Largo, Kirkton of Largo, Newburn, Colinsburgh, Kilconquhar, Earlsferry, Elie, St.Monance and Pittenweem before terminating at Anstruther. The station at Anstruther was to be sited at the harbour, on reclaimed land behind the West Pier.

As for the construction of the line, a detailed survey carried out on behalf of the promoters had found that the proposed route would not require any significant tunnelling or embanking along its entire length. The survey also pointed out that, for a six mile stretch, the route would pass along the sands lying between the villages east of Leven and would therefore not require the purchase of expensive land as well as causing the least disturbance to the countryside at these parts.

A factor concerning potential passenger traffic which was certainly not overlooked by the proposed railway company at this time was the traffic which would be generated by the already established watering places of Leven, Largo and Elie. With the coming of the railway, the number visitors travelling to these resorts would undoubtedly increase.

As well as considering the need for a railway to improve upon the established modes of transport to and from the south east corner of Fife in the mid 1800's, the new railway company had also considered the potential goods traffic that would be generated by the many mills, works, farms and fishing ports that lay along the course of the line.

At this time there existed many industries along the banks of the River Leven, including the distillery at Cameron Bridge, owned by the Haig family; and numerous spinning mills farther down the river, which would undoubtedly attract goods traffic, both in and out. The harbour at Leven was also considered at the time to be of great importance and this would have to be taken into consideration.

The farmlands of the area surrounding the River Leven and indeed the whole of the area through which the railway would pass were considered by many to be the richest and most fertile in Fife. The method used during the early part of the nineteenth century for transporting livestock and farm produce from the eastern part of the county to the markets of Edinburgh and Glasgow was by sea, incurring great cost and inconvenience. The benefits of conveying agricultural produce by rail would undoubtedly be reaped by both the local farming communities and the railway company.

The proposed terminus at Anstruther was also considered to be within easy reach of the rich agricultural lands of Crail and Kingsbarns, which were situated on the far eastern tip of Fife.

The flourishing fishing ports of Crail, Anstruther, Pittenweem and St Monance could also be relied upon to generate heavy goods traffic. Fishing was at the time the main industry and source of employment in the East Neuk, there being a very extensive trade not only in white fish, but also in herring during the summer months. As with the agricultural and livestock traffic, the only method of transporting fish to markets out with the far eastern corner of Fife had been up to this time by sea; the advantages of fast and efficient conveyance of both fish and livestock to the Glasgow, Edinburgh, Perth and Dundee markets are evident.

In addition, the cost of transporting coal and lime to the East Neuk of Fife at this time was very great and considerable financial savings could be had by transferring the carriage of these materials from sea to rail.

Taking all these factors into account, it was foreseen that investors in the railway proposed in 1845 could expect an excellent return for their money.

Alas, the proposal for a railway serving the East of Fife was considered at the time to be too ambitious, but nevertheless the seeds had been sown in the minds of the local businessmen and the construction of such a railway, or at least part of it, would not be delayed for long.

Around the same time that the original East of Fife Railway Company published its prospectus for building a railway to Anstruther, there was much talk in the north east of Fife about the possibility of connecting the university town of St Andrews with the Edinburgh, Perth and Dundee railway at Leuchars.

Unlike the proposed East of Fife Railway, whose potential revenue was expected to come equally from goods and passenger traffic, the St. Andrews Railway Company stated in their prospectus that the expected revenue generated from their railway would come mainly from passenger traffic.

The golf course at St. Andrews had long been a popular destination for the sporting gentry, the game having first been played over the famous links almost 100 years earlier. The same cannot be said about the actual town itself in the early part of the nineteenth century, however, when it is said that "filth and squalor abounded unchecked".

A report published in 1830 describes scenes of cows and pigs grazing in front of the colleges; the streets being irregular and having no side pavements and the old buildings in those streets being in a state of decay and littered with rubbish. There were few visitors to the ancient city, which was according to the report "at the lowest pitch of miserable neglect and decay".

The transformation of St Andrews began in 1832, when the town inherited a large part of the fortune of Dr Bell. Dr Bell, a native of St Andrews, had died in January of that year and had stipulated that a considerable part of his fortune of £120,000 was to go towards carrying out improvements in his native city. This resulted in the rebuilding of much of the older parts of the town; the building of MadrasCollege and the building of many new streets including the North and South Bell Streets and Playfair Terrace.

By the late 1840's the transformation of St Andrews was almost complete; the town regained its popularity with visitors, and once more became well known as a watering place along with the towns and villages on the south eastern coast of Fife.

The promoters of the new railway company anticipated that the convenience of rail travel would attract even more visitors to the town, mainly during the summer months, both for day excursions and for longer stays, to enjoy the excellent golfing and bathing facilities.

These factors, along with the guaranteed income that would be generated by the town's university, would undoubtedly generate passenger revenue. It was anticipated that this alone would amount to over £1,800 of the company's annual income. Goods traffic, however, generated mainly by the conveyance of coal, stone, tiles and farm produce would realise only half that amount. Nevertheless, the company correctly forecast that overall a handsome annual profit would be realised and the required capital was duly raised.

Construction of the first section of what was later to become the Fife Coast Line was about to begin.

B1 No.61355 pulls away from Anstruther on 21st August 1956. (A G Ellis Collection)

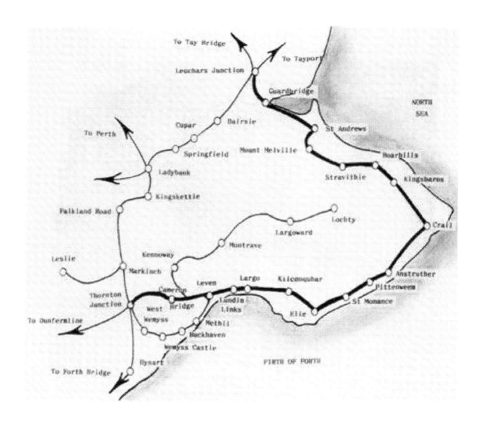

RAILWAYS IN THE EAST OF FIFE

The FifeCoast Line is depicted in bold ink.

Chapter Two
THE ST ANDREWS RAILWAY

St Andrews goods station. This was the original terminus of the St Andrews Railway when it was first opened in 1852 (Lens of Sutton).

The St Andrews Railway was first proposed in 1849, but it was not until November of the following year that an article appeared in the "Fifeshire Journal" stating that application was to be made to Parliament during the ensuing session for an Act to authorise the construction of a railway from Leuchars to St Andrews. The required capital was estimated at £21,000, with an additional £7,000 to be raised if required.

The railway was to commence from a junction with the Edinburgh, Perth and Dundee Railway near to Milton Farm in the Parish of Leuchars and terminate at or near the "sheep park" on the farm of Balgove in the Parish of St Andrews.

The railway company was to be independent from the Edinburgh, Perth and Dundee company, with whom an agreement to work the line could possibly be entered into at a later date.

As the landowners upon whose land the line would encroach had no objections to the proposals and as no major engineering difficulties were anticipated in constructing the line, the railway company immediately set about raising the necessary capital required to have the proposed Bill passed by Parliament.

A public meeting was called by the Provost of St Andrews, to be held in the Town Hall on Thursday 19th December, 1850. The purpose of the meeting was to discuss the railway company's proposals and the presence of "all those friendly to the new railway" was requested.

The meeting was well attended by numerous local businessmen, gentry and Council officials, all showing keen interest in the proposed line. The effect that the new railway would have on Council owned property was one of the topics discussed and it was unanimously resolved that the Town Council should give its assent. To show its approval of the proposed line and its appreciation of the advantages that the railway would bring to St Andrews, the Town Council duly applied for ten shares.

Less than a week later, it was announced that shares had been selling rapidly and that three quarters of the capital necessary to enable the company to apply to Parliament for an Act to allow construction of the line had already been taken up, mostly by local people. The heavy demand continued and application was made early the following year.

The St Andrews Railway Act was passed by both Houses of Parliament without objection and received Royal Sanction in July 1851.

No sooner was the railway authorised, than local residents began to air their doubts as to the suitability of the location of the St Andrews terminus, which was to be situated to the north of the town. The general feeling was that it was to be built too far from the town centre and that a far more suitable terminus could be built alongside the lifeboat shed on the opposite side of the golf links.

The main stumbling block here, however, was that the golf club would not allow their famous course to be encroached upon. It was also pointed out that such an arrangement would also pose difficulties if the line were to be continued beyond the town, due to the lie of the land. In addition, many people expressed concern that the estimated capital was insufficient.

The railway company replied that the construction costs would be kept to a minimum as the entire route along which the railway would run was flat, with the exception of a few small cuttings through clay and sand. There were to be no expensive stations and the only bridges on the line, across the River Eden and the Motray Water, were to be built from wood. The Directors had been assured that these bridges would not require maintenance for another 25 to 30 years.

As for sidings, there were to be only four. These were all to be in or around Guardbridge and were to be located at the Seggie distillery, the wharf on the River Eden, the Guardbridge Tile Works and the brick and tile works at Kincaple.

By observing the construction of many similar railways, "experience has brought wisdom", the Directors assured the shareholders, and they were confident that the line would be completed within budget.

The appointed contractor wasted little time in starting building work and the first sod was cut on the St Andrews Railway near to Guardbridge at the beginning of September 1851.

The engineer responsible for the design and construction of the line was none other than Mr Thomas Bouch, who was later to be infamously remembered for the construction of the ill-fated first TayBridge. Mr Bouch had been employed as engineer for the Edinburgh, Perth and Dundee Railway and, almost as soon as work began, he resigned from his post with the main line and set himself up as an independent consulting engineer. The St Andrews Railway was to be the first of his many commissions.

In the months following the cutting of the first sod, it appeared that the railway company had been correct in their assumption that construction would pose few problems. In March of the following year, the newspapers reported that the line was progressing rapidly and could well be finished ahead of schedule. More importantly, it was forecast that the final cost of constructing the railway could well be less than the original estimate. The company even went as far as to boast that:

"this proves that the shareholders have been particularly fortunate in their choice of Directors to whose judicious management the success of the undertaking up to this point may be fairly ascribed"

At the half yearly meeting of the company the following month, the shareholders were happy to note that the financial side of the company was healthy. The railway was now complete between St Andrews and Guardbridge and was almost complete as far as the junction with the main line at Milton. The station at St Andrews was also nearing completion.

On Tuesday 22nd June 1852, a number of spectators turned out to witness the first engine travel along the St Andrews Railway, making its way from Leuchars to St Andrews carrying an engineer's party prior to the inspection of the line by the Government Surveyor. Two days later, the Government Surveyor made the same journey and expressed himself highly satisfied with the line and "the substantial and workmanlike manner in which the whole had been executed". The line was therefore ready for opening and the official opening ceremony took place on a beautiful summer's day on Tuesday 29th June 1852.

Just before midday, the Directors boarded a train at St Andrews and proceeded to Leuchars. There they were met by deputations from Cupar, Kirkcaldy and Dunfermline, who spent several minutes congratulating the St Andrews men on their achievement. The party then returned along the line, making a brief stop to inspect the station at Guardbridge.

Between Guardbridge and St Andrews, the visiting delegation was most impressed with the view from the train. On the left was the estuary of the River Eden in full tide; on the right were the green cornfields and, looming up in the distance against the blue sky, was the impressive skyline of the ancient Cathedral City of St Andrews.

Guardbridge station in August 1956 (A.G. Ellis Collection).

The journey between Leuchars and St Andrews had taken only fifteen minutes and the smoothness and comfort of the journey was remarked on by all present.

When the train arrived back at the terminus, the official party was greeted by a band, then proceeded to march with music and banners to the Provost's house. The visiting delegation then took advantage of the opportunity to go sightseeing in St

Andrews before attending a commemorative dinner in the Town Hall at three o'clock.

Many local dignitaries attended the dinner along with the Directors and shareholders. Amongst those seated at the top table was Mr Ellice, Member of Parliament for the local burghs. Mr Ellice proposed a toast to the railway company, which was greeted with much applause. He then went on to praise the economical manner in which the line had been built, along with those responsible for its construction.

The Chairman of the railway company, Mr Smith, then proceeded to deliver a witty speech describing himself and his fellow Directors as being "very green" from the outset. They were, he said, "just like a company of young officers who had undertaken to convey a ship to a port and had rather a rum sort of crew".

Mr Smith then gave thanks to Mr Bouch the engineer and Mr Mathieson the contractor for their respective roles, despite there having been some disagreements along the way. "We are again all very good friends" said the Chairman. "Now that the ship is afloat, we hope to make a prosperous voyage of it".

Before he sat down, the Chairman had one last toast to propose. The toast was not to the St Andrews Railway, but to another railway that was, he said, only at the beginning of its difficulties. The railway he referred to would surmount its problems just as the St Andrews Railway had done and prove very beneficial to both the promoters of the railway and the County through which it would pass. He was referring to the Leven Railway.

At six o'clock, the visiting delegation made its way back to the station and boarded the train for Leuchars.

The following day, the opening of the railway to the public was commemorated with an excursion to Dunfermline and around fifty people took advantage of the offer of cheap tickets to visit the ancient Capital of Scotland.

The train left St Andrews shortly before 9 o'clock and arrived at its destination just over two hours later. The day trippers spent an enjoyable eight hours in Dunfermline, during which they were taken on a guided tour of the town. The train started back for St Andrews at 7 o'clock.

Leuchars Junction station in August 1956. The central bay platform is where the FifeCoast Line officially ended. (A.G. Ellis Collection).

Hours before the excursion party were due to arrive home, crowds began to gather at St Andrews station to await the return of the train. When the first plume of smoke from the returning engine was seen on the horizon, a loud cheer went up and, by the time the train entered the station, the police were experiencing great difficulty in keeping the enthusiastic crowd off the rails!

News of the opening of the railway to St Andrews was greeted with much enthusiasm not only in Fife, but throughout Scotland. The month of July saw three excursions visit the town from Perth, Arbroath and Glasgow; the Glasgow trip having been a "monster" one according to the local press. The following month of August saw another three visits by day trippers from Kirkcaldy, Dysart and Stirling.

The citizens of St Andrews were in no doubt that, along with the railway company, they could look forward to many prosperous years of association with the country's rail network.

Chapter Three
THE LEVEN RAILWAY

Leven Station in April 1953 (J. Robertson).

After the original proposals for the East of Fife Railway fell through in 1845, another less ambitious project to construct a railway from a junction with the Edinburgh, Perth and Dundee Railway at Thornton only as far as Leven was proposed. The line was to follow much the same route as before, with an intermediate station at Cameron Bridge; and the Leven terminus was to be constructed so as to facilitate the extension of the railway to Anstruther at a later date should the need arise.

In April 1851, the local press reported that moves were afoot to construct such a railway and in October of that year that the Leven Railway Company published its prospectus, claiming that such a railway could be constructed for £25,000 as compared with the proposed £250,000 capital quoted in the prospectus of the original East of Fife Railway.

The company stated that: *"the abandonment of the East of Fife Railway has made it clear that a less adventurous course be pursued to satisfy the more immediate requirements of the district".*

The prospectus also stated that arrangements were already in place with the Edinburgh, Perth and Dundee Railway to work the line.

General public feeling at the time was that a railway was much needed in the area, but there was a little concern amongst the inhabitants of Leven and the surrounding area that the proposals had got to such an advanced stage without public consultation. It was with this in mind that a public meeting was arranged by those responsible for promoting the railway to allay the fears of the local people.

On 16th December 1851, Sir Ralph Anstruther rose in front of a packed Gardener's Hall in Leven and delivered a lengthy speech praising the efforts of certain public spirited individuals who had taken a most active part in surveying, planning and estimating the cost of the proposed line. In answer to those who felt that a public meeting was long overdue, he said that the object of the meeting was to arrive at some clear and practical result and if a meeting had been called before the company had chalked out a line of procedure then such a meeting would have defeated instead of promoted the railway. In not calling a meeting until all the facts were known, they were not treating the public with disrespect, but with the utmost respect and consideration.

Sir Ralph's speech also emphasised the need for a railway. It was his observation that towns connected to the railway network prospered, while those without a railway made no progress and saw the stream of traffic which had formerly passed their doors diverted into other channels. He also claimed that members of the public had shown a desire to reside in towns where railway communications existed. With this in mind he went on to say:

"Now as I presume that you have no inclination to quit this sunny side of the hill and migrate to Markinch, to the higher ground and colder climate, or to add another mile or two to the long town of Kirkcaldy, I think you will be glad if you can bring these advantages to your own doors".

Mr John Haig, owner of the distillery at CameronBridge and Chairman of the railway company, also addressed the meeting. It was his opinion that the anticipated railway traffic would be greatly increased if the line were to be taken down to the harbour at Leven instead of terminating at Burnmill, on the north side of the town. This further extension of the line could be built for an additional £2,500; which, he said, would complete the railway "from sea to sea", providing a continuous line of rails from Leven to Greenock, "the advantages of which were at once apparent". This was greeted with much applause from the assembly.

The meeting was wound up with an appeal for support for the railway. The company had to raise £15,000 before 31st December 1851 to allow the Leven Railway Bill to be presented to Parliament. So far £12,500 had been raised, leaving the company £2,500 short. The company, therefore, had only two weeks left to raise the necessary capital and it was hoped that the people of Leven would take a small number of shares to enable the Bill to be heard.

Those towns lying to the east of Leven, it was claimed, also had a particular interest in the railway, as the benefits of rail travel would bring the larger cities of Scotland within easier reach of the East Neuk of Fife's farming and fishing industries. The company therefore appealed to the "intelligent and industrious cultivators of the land" and to the "array of able, gallant and hearty fishermen" of those communities lying to the east of Leven to come forward and take up a small number of shares, bearing in mind that it was only a matter of time before the line would be extended to reach the towns of Elie and Anstruther.

The company were happy to report a short time later that the undertaking was ready for the Sanction of Parliament.

The company appointed a certain Mr Bouch as its engineer and went to great lengths to point out that in doing so they had engaged an engineer who was held in the highest esteem for his part in the construction of the Edinburgh, Perth and Dundee Railway.

Preserved Class 5 No.44871 'Sovereign' passes Leven as it returns from a special trip to the power station in Methil in 1991 (Author's Collection).

Sir Ralph Anstruther claimed that Bouch had drawn up the most beautiful plans for the Leven Railway and, taking into account the interest that the engineer had shown in the project, it was Sir Ralph's opinion that the company would have gone far before they would have found one better qualified for the duties Mr Bouch had undertaken. It would appear, however, that in reality Bouch had been appointed on the grounds that he could construct a railway at a cost of around £4,000 per mile compared with the Scottish average cost of £31,000 per mile!

Mr Bouch himself had stated publicly that: *"The failure in railways was the excessive waste in capital in their construction. The best paying lines were not those that got the most traffic, but those that had been constructed at least expense".*

Twenty seven years later, after having been knighted by Queen Victoria only the previous year, Sir Thomas Bouch was to regret his policy of construction using the most economical means when his Tay Bridge collapsed on 28th December 1879 killing seventy- nine people.

As the weeks went by, the Leven Railway Company went from strength to strength as the shares were bought up and the full amount of capital required for the construction of the line was realised.

CameronBridge station on August 23rd 1953 (J. Robertson).

Not everyone, however, was full of enthusiasm for the railway. A most vociferous and active opponent was Mr C M Christie of Durie, who tried everything in his power to try to stop construction of the line. In a letter to the "Fife Journal" dated 12th February 1852, he called upon the people of Leven to object to the Leven Railway Bill on the grounds that the proposed level crossings on the two northern entrances into the town would present a great danger to the public. He stated that he did not think the local inhabitants had "contemplated the annoyance, interruption and danger to which the communication betwixt Leven and the interior of the county will be permanently subjected". He went on to say that they should "observe how impossible it will be to get rid of this evil after the railway has been completed".

Christie's fight with the railway did not end there. Not only did he stand in the way of the railway company at every opportunity, he also demanded a ridiculous sum of compensation where the railway was to cross his land. The railway company had no option but to allow a jury to decide on the amount of payment due. Unfortunately for Mr Christie, Parliament and local juries who only a few years previously had been opposed to the construction of railways, had began to lean towards the railway companies. The outcome was that the jury awarded Mr Christie less than the railway company had originally offered!

The Leven Railway Bill was passed by the Committee of the House of Commons in April 1852, but not without further opposition. As well as from Christie of Durie, petitions were also received from two other local landowners and a certain group of individuals calling themselves the "Trustees of the LevenBridge and Road". The objectors claimed that the railway would be injurious to their estates as well as being unnecessary.

Two of the protests were withdrawn before the House of Commons Committee met, and the petition from the Leven Bridge Trustees was thrown out as it was claimed that the gentlemen had no "locus standi".

One landowner, however, decided to further his case for opposition by appealing to the House of Lords. This further appeal was also rejected and the Leven Railway Bill eventually became an Act of Parliament on 17th June, 1852.

Construction of the line began in the summer of 1852 and before long it became clear that the difficulties endured by the company in trying to get the Bill through Parliament was only the start of their troubles. As well as having received a hostile reception from certain landowners upon whose land the railway was to be built, the railway company soon began to regret appointing Thomas Bouch as its engineer.

Mr Bouch had been held in high esteem by the promoters of the railway, who had publicly praised him for the plans he had drawn up and the interest he had shown in the line when it was first proposed. Almost as soon as construction work was started, however, it became apparent that the engineer was not as reliable as the company had thought. He failed to produce plans when requested and, of the plans he did produce, there were frequent inaccuracies and miscalculations. Throughout the entire two years that it took to build the line, Mr Bouch frequently failed to reply to letters from the secretary of the railway company and failed to attend important meetings.

Despite these shortcomings, the company honoured the appointment of the infamous engineer, not realising that many of the mistakes he had made in designing the line were not to come to light until after the railway was opened!

As the months went by, the Leven Railway slowly began to take shape and all along the banks of the rivers Ore and Leven could heard the sound of the railway navvies toiling away with pick and shovel as the line wound its way down from Thornton.

Sadly, accidents and injuries to the navvies were commonplace, there being almost a total disregard to safe working practices by railway contractors during the nineteenth century. In the months leading up to the completion of building work, the local press had occasion to report on two serious accidents on the line in the space of one week. Near to CameronBridge on Saturday May 13th 1854, a deaf and dumb mute was struck by a runaway wagon. As well as having a serious head wound, the poor man had to have his foot amputated as a result. The following Wednesday there was a more serious mishap when an embankment collapsed, causing a "weighty portion" of earth to fall on a workman, whose injuries were to prove fatal.

After several postponements, the Leven Railway eventually opened on Saturday 5th August 1854. The occasion was celebrated by the Directors, shareholders and others connected with the railway taking a trip from Leven to Thornton in a special train of seven coaches.

The train was headed by a beautiful new engine which had been delivered from Edinburgh only the day before and whose nameplate was proudly emblazoned with the words "Leven Railway". As the engine made its way along the banks of the River Leven and past CameronBridge, the official party were cheered by enthusiastic handkerchief waving crowds. Heading on towards Thornton, the scene is perhaps best described by this report taken from the following edition of the "Fifeshire Advertiser":

"In that once lovely vale, where the hare and rabbit sunned themselves undisturbed, a crowded train now rattles along leaving a trail of smoke behind and instead of the call of the wood pigeon, the shrill cry of the lapwing, or the song of the linnet, can be heard the tramp of the iron steed, the snort of the puffing engine and the sound of the railway whistle."

In the evening, after the jubilant entourage had returned to Leven, a splendid dinner was served up to an assembly of about sixty gentlemen in Crawford's Hotel in celebration of the event. Flushed with success, the Chairman of the company, John Haig, sat at the top table accompanied by Sir Ralph Anstruther. So proud were they of their achievement and so confident were they that the line was destined to succeed, that only three weeks later a meeting was called to discuss the extension of the line to Anstruther. The iron steed was tramping forth.

Chapter Four
THE EAST OF FIFE RAILWAY

Lundin Links station on August 23rd 1956 (A.G. Ellis Collection).

After the opening of the Leven Railway in 1854, it was inevitable that the thriving fishing communities of the East Neuk of Fife would not be kept off the railway map for long.

The herring fishing industry was thriving in the area during the middle part of the nineteenth century. The Lammas Drave, which was the name given to the herring fishing which took place off the eastern coast of Fife during the months of August and September, was at its peak. The fish which was landed at the East Neuk ports at that time could only find its way to the southern fish markets by way of steamer to Leith and from there by rail to the English buyers.

Potential fish traffic, along with the anticipated agricultural traffic that would be generated from the rich farmlands of the area, were major factors in the railway promoters' favour and, in due course, the East of Fife Railway was incorporated by an Act of Parliament on the 23rd of July 1855.

It was proposed at this time to take the railway only as far as Kilconquhar, with the extension to Anstruther to be constructed at some future date.

The engineer appointed by the company was once again Thomas Bouch. Soon after his appointment, however, his miscalculations concerning the building of the Leven Railway were beginning to come to light. Bearing in mind the trouble that Mr Bouch had given the Leven Company during the construction of its railway, the East of Fife company decided that he should be replaced. The engineer appointed in his place was Bouch's assistant, Mr Martin.

The viaduct across the Kiel Burn at Largo was "an object of considerable beauty" according to the Fifeshire Advertiser in 1857 (C.W.R. Bowman).

Construction then began and the line was opened as far as Lundin Mill for goods traffic in February 1857.

In March of that year, the "Fifeshire Advertiser" reported that the benefits of the railway were greatly appreciated by the public and that the construction of the line to the east, including the viaduct over the Kiel Burn at Largo, was well under way. The line was also to be opened for passenger traffic in the near future.

Two months later, the same newspaper claimed that the opening of the railway along its entire extent to Kilconquhar was imminent. It is also interesting to note that this edition, dated 9th May 1857, claimed that:

"The viaduct across the vale near the harbour of Lower Largo is now an object of considerable beauty and its utility will soon be felt to the advantage of the public".

On Friday 31st July 1857, large crowds gathered to see an engine make a trial run along the line as far as Kilconquhar. Later that afternoon, a large party of shareholders and their friends dined together in celebration of the event. The dinner was chaired by John Haig Esq., Chairman of the Leven Railway, who was happy to report that the line was one of the smoothest in the country and a great credit to both the engineer and contractor.

On 11th August 1857, the East of Fife Railway was opened to passenger and goods traffic, and within a month the line was hailed as a huge success, with passenger ticket sales for the first few weeks of operation reported to have exceeded all expectations, with 575 tickets sold in the first five days alone.

The following week 940 people travelled on the line and this was followed by 895 passengers during the week ending 29th August, excluding the return tickets sold in Edinburgh during this period. Goods traffic was also reported to be favourable and it was anticipated that this would increase as the season advanced.

At the half yearly meeting of the company, held in Leven in October 1857, Chairman Sir Ralph Anstruther was happy to report that the traffic on the railway was very promising. The line had conveyed an average of 947 passengers per week, a figure that had exceeded all estimations. An agreement to work the line jointly with the Leven Railway was recommended by the Directors.

On 22nd July 1861 the East of Fife Railway was amalgamated with the Leven Railway under the Leven and East of Fife Railway Act.

An early postcard photograph of Kilconquhar station, which was the terminus of the East of Fife Railway for six years (Lens of Sutton).

At this time, passengers from Anstruther and the East Neuk wishing to make use of the new railway line had to board a horse drawn coach which departed from Anstruther four times daily to connect with the trains at Kilconquhar. Despite the fact that Anstruther lay only six miles beyond the rail terminus, this journey took over an hour. Connection between Anstruther and Crail could be had by making use of "Mrs M's Mail Gig", according to an advertisement in the "East of Fife Record" at the time.

The stock was duly taken up as anticipated and construction of the line commenced.

Progress, however, was slow. Soon it became apparent that the new railway would not reach Anstruther as quickly as Mr Oliphant had anticipated, much to the vexation of the locals. Newspaper reports complaining about the time taken to construct the six mile stretch were frequent, claiming that construction had not been held up by bad weather or for any other reason.

The East of Fife Railway was, however, finally opened to Anstruther on September 1st 1863. After several days of heavy rain, which had seen the roof of the new engine shed at the terminus give way in several places, the weather improved somewhat and the opening took place on a pleasant day, rather surprisingly without ceremony.

A considerable crowd gathered during the day to witness the "novelty of a railway in operation", but the number of people who actually boarded the three trains which departed from the station that day was disappointing, however, with only 150 passengers being carried. Of these, a large proportion was reported to be fishermen who did not stay locally, returning from the sea to their homes and families in the Highlands and Borders.

Those who did use the line on the first few days of operation reported most favourably on what they had experienced. The substantial way in which the railway had been constructed was commented on and the journey was found to be exceedingly smooth; there being no "jarring or jolting so frequently met with on railways".

Mr Oliphant's "steam horse" had begun its 102 year association with the East Neuk.

*Anstruther Station in the 1960's with a Diesel Multiple Unit (DMU)
preparing to depart for Edinburgh (Author's Collection)*

Chapter Five

EARLY DAYS

A Leven and East of Fife Railway timetable from October 1857

The effect that the coming of the railways had on the one-time isolated communities which they served was at once apparent. Before long, the towns and villages on the Fife coast began to be visited by people from all walks of life in pursuit of various pastimes.

The initial success of the St Andrews Railway has already been described in an earlier chapter. On the Leven Railway the story was much the same, with the Directors happy to report not long after the line had opened that passenger and goods traffic had far exceeded all expectations.

In his "Handy Book of the Fife Coast", published in the early 1860's, Henry Farnie describes in great detail the effect that the Leven Railway had on the town in the very early years of operation, when during the summer there would be a large influx of visitors from the cities; visitors who were totally unaccustomed to the ways of the sea and seashore, as is described in this paragraph taken from the book:

"In the summer months you only have to saunter down to Leven Sands to know that its merits are beginning to be known to the world at large. He who through the rest of the year has been pursuing his avocation with all the eagerness of monomania, or who has been so absorbed in fashion or in study that gas light and sun light constituted the only vicissitude in the external world, is now seen plodding along the shore in the attitude of childhood, busying himself in the mysteries of shells and seaweed, or marking with solicitude the advance of the tide over some stone in which he has compelled himself, from some vacancy of thought, to feel a degree of interest. Here you see, in a crazy boat, some learned professor in company with an old fisherman, casting their lines in Largo Bay, eager in quest of flounders - there you see a venerable judge in fierce contest with a crab, which he is endeavouring with his silver headed cane to wrench from its "coy abode"".

The railway caused Leven to become popular not only as a destination for day trippers and holidaymakers but also as a desirable place of residence. In the late 1850's and 1860's the town grew rapidly to the east, with many handsome villas being constructed, no doubt as a direct result of better transport communications with the rest of the country.

As well as making Leven a more accessible place for people from other areas, the railway made it possible for the residents of Leven to visit other towns and cities. Shortly after the railway came to the town, the local townsfolk, tired of working six days a week in the mills and factories amidst the dirt, dust and noise of machinery, decided that it was about time they had an annual holiday. It was decided that the first such holiday was to be on Thursday 7th September, 1854.

From early in the morning, crowds of excursionists made their way to the station, intent on exploring some seemingly far off destination that had suddenly been made accessible to them by the advent of the railway train. Some decided to visit Edinburgh, but the majority decided to make use of a cheap excursion ticket to Perth, where by all accounts the day trippers had a thoroughly enjoyable day out. The massed exodus was so big that Leven took on "the aspect and air of a deserted town" according to the local newspaper. When the happy and carefree crowds returned in the evening, there was a general feeling of satisfaction and contentment with the events of the day. "A general holiday is a blessing - and the convenience of railways is equally so", claimed the following edition of the "Fifeshire Advertiser".

Not everyone, though, was thrilled at the sight and sound of a train steaming along the line. A newspaper report in October 1854 tells of a gentleman on horseback who was riding alongside the railway on his way to visit some friends in Windygates. As he was passing CameronBridge, a train went "snorting past" and startled the horse, which went darting off at speed. The poor gentleman became unseated and was left nursing a severely bruised posterior!

The early success of the Leven Railway was eventually matched by the success of the extension of the East of Fife line to Anstruther. George Gourlay, in his book simply entitled "Anstruther", published in 1888, informs the visitor to the town by rail that the best time to come and see the railway in operation was in the spring.

Visitors to the town at that time of year could expect to witness the departure of:

"A hundred wagons of caller herrin', jist new drawn frae the firth, to every city and market town in merrie England".

The original passenger terminus at Anstruther. The station buildings remained intact until final closure of the line in 1965! (A.G. Ellis Collection).

The early days of the railway in Anstruther were also recalled many years later in a series of articles printed in Anstruther's weekly newspaper, the "East Fife Observer".

The articles were written by eighty-year-old William Smith, who had resided in Cellardyke until deciding, at an early age, to seek his fortune out with the bounds of his native town. The year that "Auld Wull" left Cellardyke was 1863, the same year that the East of Fife line was opened to Anstruther. "The station was at West Anstruther then and long after, till the railway came to Crail", recalled Wull.

The article goes on to describe how the young William Smith had made his way to the station and asked the Station Master, James Brown, for a ticket to Leith. "How old are ye?" enquired the voice from the ticket office. "Fourteen" answered the enterprising youngster. "You're no very big" said the Station Master - "We'll let ye for half a ticket".

James Brown had been the agent for the steamer that had at that time plied between Anstruther and Leith. It was William Smith's opinion that the railway company had appointed Mr Brown as Station Master in an attempt to capture the shipping company's trade!

Early days in the East Neuk: North British 0-6-0 No.190 poses outside Anstruther engine shed at the turn of the 20th century (Author's collection).

Those early days of operation were not, however, all plain sailing for the St Andrews and Leven companies, largely due to one person; the infamous Thomas Bouch!

Both companies were slowly coming to realise that Mr Bouch's inexpensive railway construction practices were causing major problems in both the running and maintenance of their railways.

In the case of the St Andrews Railway, the line had been constructed using a lighter rail than was generally accepted as standard and the sleepers had been placed too far apart. As a result, only the lightest engines were able to use the line, which meant that only light loads could be carried.

Another major headache for the St Andrews company was the deteriorating condition of the two bridges over the River Eden and the Motray Water. It transpired that Mr Bouch had constructed the bridges using inferior material and had decided that the use of any kind of preservative was unnecessary, at the same time assuring the Directors of the St Andrews company that maintenance would not be required for some 20 to 30 years!

North British 0-6-0 No.142 at Anstruther shed in 1900 (Author's collection).

On the Leven Railway, the mistake made by the man who some had once regarded as "the greatest railway engineer in the country" was even more remarkable. The engine that Mr Bouch had ordered for the Leven company was one which would be able to negotiate the curves and gradients on the line as originally designed. What the engineer had forgotten to take into account, however, was the short cuts and cost cutting measures that had been taken in actually constructing the railway.

It therefore turned out that the engine was unable to negotiate most of the curves on the line safely when travelling even at a moderate speed and this resulted in the engine having to travel so slowly that the service became intolerable.

The days of the small railway companies, however, were numbered. No matter how successful they were, it was inevitable that they would eventually be bought out by one of the bigger fish that swept through the country swallowing up the smaller fry during the latter part of the nineteenth century.

In the case of the Leven and East of Fife and the St Andrews companies, this fish took the form of the North British Railway; and both companies were absorbed by the North British on 1st August 1877 under the North British Railway (Amalgamations) Act of 28th June 1877.

Under the new parent company, with whom the line would be associated for almost half a century, the success story of the revenue generated by the East Neuk fishing industry continued. Throughout the late 1800's the station at Anstruther was alive with the clatter of horses hooves entering the station yard pulling fully laden fish carts, mingled with the sound of railway engines arriving and departing. Newspaper reports of the time tell of almost 300 fully laden wagons of herring leaving the station in a single day.

Back down the line at Leven, the railway was also well patronised during the latter part of the last century.

Amongst the wide and varied goods traffic which was generated by the various industries within the town, was the transport of considerable quantities of yarn. Bleaching of yarn was carried out on a very large scale in Leven in the 1890's, the yarn being brought in by rail from such places as Dundee and Arbroath as well as from many factories within Fife.

LevenHarbour and Methil docks, though, were probably the greatest sources of revenue for the railway company towards the end of the nineteenth century. The advantages that John

Haig had claimed to be apparent when he first proposed to take the railway down to the harbour at Leven were now being enjoyed by the North British. The big fish was digesting its prey.

Chapter Six
HARBOUR BRANCH LINES

One route proposed for the Anstruther harbour branch was to follow the route of the Dreel Burn by suspending the rails over the water (Author's collection).

It is rather surprising that a once busy fishing port such as Anstruther should have had no direct harbour rail connection, but in fact there were three such proposals.

The first of these came in 1845 as part of the prospectus for the original East of Fife Railway, which stated that the proposed line from Thornton would terminate "at the Harbour of Anstruther." It was intended that this railway would reach the shore by following the course of the Dreel Burn, and a passenger station was to be built on the West Sands at the rear of the present West Pier.

The idea of having a railway down to the harbour again cropped up in 1866, when the construction of the UnionHarbour at Anstruther was commenced. The prospect of having improved shipping facilities in the town inspired the Leven and East of Fife Railway Company, along with the Harbour Commissioners, to look at the possibility of constructing a branch line from the station down to the new harbour.

It is perhaps significant that the Lammas Drave herring fishing, which took place off the east coast of Fife, had peaked in 1860 and no doubt the Harbour Commissioners anticipated similarly heavy fish landings in the years to come. To connect the harbour with the railway system would speed the transit of fish to the markets of the larger towns and cities and would therefore be a great advantage to the local fishing community.

As well as the business that could be gained from fish traffic, the railway company also wished to exploit the great potential revenue that lay in the export of coal from the East Neuk port. The mining of coal in Fife during the mid nineteenth century was rapidly increasing and, in the 1860's, the only major Fife ports engaged in the export of coal were Burntisland and Tayport.

In 1868 a feasibility survey was carried out and, as a result, two possible routes from the station to the harbour were proposed. The most economical route, which could be built at an estimated cost of £4,065, was to extend the railway from its terminus in West Anstruther by way of a bridge over the Anstruther to Pittenweem road. The line would then run down the lane which is today known as Crichton Street, then cut through the gardens at the rear of the houses on the south side of West High Street before crossing the beach and terminating on the pier-head.

The second route, which was to cost £5,370, was to branch off from the north of the station and cross the Dreel Burn and the West Anstruther Bleaching Green, then run along the rear of the houses on the north side of West High Street.

The proposition was that this railway would then follow the exact course of the Dreel Burn and would be suspended over it by way of wooden or iron girders. The final approach to the harbour was to be made by cutting off a portion of the churchyard and also by demolishing DreelCastle.

The engineer responsible for surveying this route had calculated that there would be sufficient room for railway wagons to pass under the existing road bridge across the Dreel, but the wagons would have to be horse-drawn as there was insufficient clearance for an engine. This problem, though, could be overcome by constructing a new road bridge over the burn a little further upstream.

The proposed road bridge was to form an extension of the lane that today runs down to the old ford at the rear of the Dreel Tavern and, if constructed, would have eliminated the notorious "Buckie House Corner" at the junction of West High Street and Elizabeth Place.

There was, however, one condition laid down by the railway company. The new branch line would only be constructed if the Harbour Commissioners would agree to the construction of a wet dock, where ships could load and unload at all states of the tide. The railway company estimated that if such a dock were to be constructed, then at least 1500 tons of coal could be shipped from Anstruther weekly.

Without the assurance that the new Union Harbour would be "so constructed as to afford the fullest facility for shipping and unshipping of goods", the construction of the harbour branch could not begin; and it did not.

In 1911, proposals were once again drawn up for the construction of a branch line to Anstruther harbour, this time by the North British Railway Company. Unlike the 1868 proposals, this line was to diverge from the main line at a point midway between Anstruther and Pittenweem, near to the farm at Milton Muir.

Curving round to head south, the line was to pass under the Anstruther to Pittenweem road by way of a tunnel, which was to emerge on the south side of the road at a point behind where the houses which form St Adrian's Place were later to be built.

After crossing the golf course, the railway would reach the shore near to the present day golf clubhouse. From here the line would run along the rear of the houses in Shore Road as far as the old West Anstruther pier, where it would curve round and pass to the front of Castle Street, before reaching the harbour. If necessary, the line could be extended from this point along Shore Street as far as the lifeboat shed.

The area behind the west pier at Anstruther could have become a vast and derelict former railway yard if the 1911 proposals to construct a branch line to the harbour had materialised! (Author's collection).

Between the golf clubhouse and the harbour, a land reclamation project was to be undertaken so as to allow the installation of siding accommodation for the storage of fish wagons.

This ambitious project, though, went the way of its predecessors, which is probably just as well considering the scar that could today have been left on the picturesque seafront at Anstruther!

The herring fishing industry in the east of Fife started to go into decline after the Second World War, and with it went any prospect of there ever being a branch line down to AnstrutherHarbour. One can only wonder if we might today have had a vast and derelict former railway yard at the rear of the west pier such as can be seen at many locations in Fife today.

Preserved Class 5 No. 44871 "Sovereign" steams up the former Leven harbour branch in September 1991 (Author's collection).

The only harbour railway that ever branched off from the Fife Coast Line was that which served the harbour at Leven and extended over the river to serve the docks at Methil. This mile-long branch was first proposed by the Chairman of the Leven Railway Company along with the original Leven Railway proposals in 1851, but was not actually constructed until the harbour at Leven was converted to form a wet dock in the late 1870's.

At the opening of the Leven Railway in August 1854, the gentleman who had proposed that the line should be taken down to the harbour expressed his disappointment that this had not materialised. In his speech, made at the dinner to commemorate the opening, the Chairman lamented:

"There have been some points of difference with the Directors of the main line, who seemed to think that if the line was extended to the harbour it would act as a sucker instead of a feeder to the main line".

When the Leven Harbour Company was formed in 1877 with a view to improving the limited facilities that existed for the loading and unloading of ships at the mouth of the River Leven, proposals were again put forward that the railway be extended to the harbour.

The line was to take a course down the north bank of the river before passing under the turnpike road leading to the BawbeeBridge. As the line emerged from the tunnel under the road and entered the harbour area, sidings were to fan out and run along the piers.

Construction of the new harbour took just over two years to complete. In April 1879, the company held its half yearly shareholders meeting in the Caledonian Hotel and were able to report to those present that:

"The works on the railway branch from the Leven and East of Fife Railway to the turnpike road bridge are nearly completed. On the whole the works are progressing favourably".

The Directors of the harbour company also stated that an agreement to work the line had been reached with the North British Railway Company.

By the following spring the harbour was fully operational and before long the port of Leven began to export coal from the Fife coal fields to destinations as far distant as France and Norway.

"Business is looking quite brisk at the new dock", reported the "Fifeshire Journal", who went on to say that Leven looked like becoming a large thriving seaport town.

The quantities of coal being exported from the Fife coal fields continued to rise during the 1880's and very soon even the new dock at Leven proved to be too small to cope with the ever increasing demand. Across the other side of the River Leven, the small harbour at Methil was also experiencing difficulty handling the volumes of coal exported from the Wemyss Estate. This ultimately resulted in the construction of Methil Docks by the Wemyss Coal Company.

In order to remove the threat of competition and opposition to his new dock, Randolph Wemyss entered into negotiations to buy the Leven Harbour Company. This purchase was completed in 1887, the same year that the first dock at Methil was opened.

The harbour branch was then extended over the River Leven to serve the new dock at Methil, which was also connected by rail to the collieries of the Wemyss Estate by the Thornton to Methil branch line, opened in 1884. As Methil Docks thrived, LevenHarbour went into decline and fell into disrepair. It was eventually filled in with waste from the Wemyss pits.

When the No.3 dock was opened at Methil in 1913, the railway that had originally been built as the Leven Harbour Branch Line was quadrupled to cope with the ever increasing volumes of coal being exported from Methil docks.

During the 1920's and 1930's, Methil Docks also generated considerable rail traffic in the form of fish trains from the East Neuk; the fish being brought to Methil to be loaded on to ships for export to the Continent, with Germany a particularly popular destination.

The harbour branch was still in use until fairly recently, serving Methil Power Station. The track-bed of the line around to Methil docks is also extant, although the rails have now been lifted.

The railway sidings on the site of the former harbour at Leven survived until the area was cleared in the mid 1980's to allow construction of the Levenmouth Swimming Pool and Sports Centre.

Class 37 "Clydesmill" returning from Methil Power Station up the former LevenHarbour branch line in 1995. The engine is passing where the Methil Docks line branched off; the track from that section, as the photo suggests, already having been removed.
(Author's Collection)

Chapter Seven

THE ANSTRUTHER AND ST ANDREWS RAILWAY

"Enjoy the fresh air" advises the poster in this undated view of Anstruther station. This station replaced the old terminus in 1883, shortly after the railway was extended to Boarhills (Author's collection).

Despite the early success of the St Andrews, Leven and East of Fife Railways, it was not until the late 1870's that proposals were put forward to link Anstruther with St Andrews and complete the route around the Fife coast. The proposed railway was to start from Anstruther and head eastwards towards Crail. From here, the line was to head north towards St Andrews, with stations at Kingsbarns, Boarhills, Stravithie and MountMelville. The expected cost of the new railway was estimated at around £45,000.

At a meeting held on 28th July 1879 by those responsible for promoting the railway, statistics relating to the omnibus traffic that existed at that time between Anstruther, St Andrews and Crail were considered. If the passenger figures were correct, then prospective shareholders in the new venture could expect a reasonable return on their investments. The goods

47

traffic on the line was also expected to generate considerable revenue, as the railway was to pass through what the promoters regarded as being "the best agricultural district in Fife". There were also several quarries operating near to the proposed sixteen mile route.

The Secretary of the Provisional Committee which was set up to promote the new Anstruther and St Andrews Railway was Mr Oliphant, the same gentleman who had been responsible for raising the capital required to bring the railway to Anstruther almost two decades earlier.

In 1878, Mr Oliphant approached the North British Railway Company, who by this time had absorbed both the Leven and East of Fife Railway and the St Andrews Railway, to ask if the North British would be willing to form junctions with the proposed line at both Anstruther and St Andrews.

The response from the North British was most favourable. Not only would the company move their present station at St Andrews to a new site nearer to the town centre, where a junction could be formed, they were also willing to assist with the construction of a new through station at Anstruther.

Mr Stirling, Chairman of the North British, did however recommend that the new company should delay proceedings for about a year until more positive steps had been taken by his company with a view to relocating the St Andrews station.

Little or no objection was received from the landowners along the line and all seemed to be going well until the latter part of 1879, when grave doubts were expressed by the people of St Andrews over the sincerity of the North British Railway's proposals for the new station at St Andrews. In addition to this, there was much concern as to the location of the proposed new station and as to whether or not a junction would be made with the new line from Anstruther.

On Monday 26th January 1880, a stormy public meeting was held in St AndrewsTown Hall; the meeting having been called by the Town Council to discuss the concerns of the local people.

Councillor Paterson, in expressing the concern felt by himself, his fellow Councillors and the many shareholders who were present, put forward a resolution:

"That any scheme to construct a railway between St Andrews and Anstruther is unsatisfactory which does not provide for a junction with the station at St Andrews."

The resolution was seconded by Mr W C Henderson, who added that if the new railway from Anstruther were to terminate at any place other than at a junction with the North British line then it would be "very inconvenient for passengers travelling from north to south to have to walk between the two stations".

Mr Oliphant replied and informed the meeting that he had, indeed, approached the Town Council some months earlier with a petition which he had wished to put before the North British Railway Company.

The purpose of this petition was to express the concerns of the local inhabitants regarding the present location of the station and to seek assurance from the North British that they would honour their proposal to move the St Andrews station nearer to the town, from where a junction with the line to Anstruther could be made.

"What did the Town Council do?" asked Mr Oliphant. "Did they go heartily into this? Did they sign the petition? No! They pooh-poohed it and cast it over the table!"

Looking north from St Andrews towards Leuchars (Lens of Sutton).

Mr Oliphant proposed that his petition should still be presented to the North British company, although there was little doubt in his mind that the company had up till now acted fairly. It was his view that the line would indeed be extended into the centre of the town in due course. Whether or not Mr Oliphant's petition was presented to the North British is unclear, but one can imagine the company's response if it was. The TayBridge disaster was only four weeks old at the time and the North British Railway Company would have had more to worry about than the small matter of forming a junction with a railway that had still to leave the drawing board!

As to the idea that the new railway would terminate at its own station with no through connection with the North British line to Leuchars, Mr Oliphant assured the assembly that such an arrangement would only be a temporary one until such a connection could be made.

If the North British Railway were to change their minds about ever forming a junction with the new line, then it was proposed that the Anstruther and St Andrews Railway would terminate to the south of the city at Cairnsmill (which is where

MountMelville station was eventually built). From here the railway could be connected with the North British network by taking one of a number of alternative routes, completely bypassing St Andrews.

The mood of the meeting and indeed the general attitude of certain inhabitants of St Andrews are perhaps best summed up by the editorial comments in the "Fifeshire Journal", which stated:

"Some people in St Andrews are of the opinion that unless they can have the entire loaf they will have no bread. They will not have a railway to Anstruther from St Andrews unless the junction is made at once in the scheme."

The capital required for the construction of the line was realised by the summer of 1880 and the Anstruther and St Andrews Railway Bill was presented to Parliament in August of that year.

On the 26th of August 1880, the Bill became an Act of Parliament, and the railway company immediately set about the task of appointing a contractor. The successful applicant was William Orr Coghill of Inverness, who estimated that his company could construct the proposed line in approximately eighteen months at a cost of £38,000 plus an additional £18,000 for the cost of the rails. As the actual amount of capital raised by the company was £57,000, the railway company assumed that it had sufficient funds to cover all expenses. Mr John Buchanan, C.E., of Edinburgh, was subsequently appointed as engineer.

The construction of the railway was seen as being a relatively straightforward task; the biggest problems being the construction of the viaducts over the Kinness Burn at St Andrews, the Kenly Water at Boarhills and the Dreel Burn at Anstruther. The construction of the other seventeen bridges on the line and the laying of the track itself were expected to be fairly straightforward. Construction work was scheduled to start in the spring of 1881.

On Wednesday 13th April 1881, visitors to Anstruther were greeted with the sight of most of the local public buildings adorned with bunting to commemorate the cutting of the first sod. At one o'clock, a crowd of several hundred people made their way to a field situated to the north of the Anstruther terminus, where the ceremony was to take place.

The honour of cutting the first sod was given to Mrs Purvis, wife of the Chairman of the railway company. Mr Coghill, the contractor, presented Mrs Purvis with a "beautiful silver shovel" and the Chairman's wife proceeded to carry out her honorary task before tossing the piece of turf into the cheering crowd. The officials then made their way to AnstrutherTown Hall, where a banquet of cake and wine awaited.

The construction of the line did not run as smoothly as had been anticipated, however. Despite claims by the contractor that he would have the railway completed in eighteen months, progress was slow and, by the time the summer of 1882 arrived, only about a quarter of the line had been completed. Then came the news that the contractor was experiencing financial difficulties, not only with this undertaking, but with several projects throughout Scotland. The consequence was that contractor William Orr Coghill ultimately had to declare himself bankrupt. This inevitably resulted in work on the line being completely suspended for several months until a successor could be found.

Throughout these setbacks, though, one major problem lay unresolved; the junction with the St Andrews Railway and the construction of a joint station nearer to the centre of St Andrews. The North British, it would seem, were still dragging their heels over the matter.

At the half yearly meeting of the shareholders at the end of October 1882, the announcement was made that the engineer had recommended the abandonment of the proposals for the joint station at Argyle Street. If the cost of such a station, estimated to be around £3,000, was to be borne by the Anstruther and St Andrews company, then it would probably be better if the railway were to be extended to form a junction with the North British line at the original terminus at a cost of around £6,000. The reason behind this latest proposal was that the company felt it would be better to have a junction with the North British at a point outside the town than have no junction at all.

The estimated cost of extending the line to meet the original St Andrews Railway did, however, allow for the construction of a small station at the WestPort, between Argyle Street and Double Dykes Road. This small station, which would consist of one platform and a small ticket office, would enable the railway company to compete with the 'bus service.

"If 'buses could set people down in the centre of town, then the railway must do so also", claimed Mr Oliphant the Secretary. "If we carry them three quarters of a mile past St Andrews on a snowy, rainy day, they will go instead for the 'bus".

The Directors therefore resolved to make application to Parliament for authorisation to continue the line from the previously proposed terminus to a junction with the North British at the present St Andrews terminus. The North British, seeing that their chance to move closer to the town centre was slipping from their grasp, quickly resolved their differences with the Anstruther and St Andrews company, and early the following year an agreement was reached between the two companies to build a joint station nearer to the centre of St Andrews.

Meanwhile, with a new contractor now in place, the Directors were able to report to the shareholders that "work has restarted vigorously" on the line.

The labourers (or "navvies", as they were more commonly known) who were hired by the new contractor were accommodated in a bothy known as the "Caiplie Hut", which was situated near to the line between Anstruther and Crail. Conditions in the Caiplie Hut, which could sleep about forty men, were very cramped and the bothy was likened to the "steerage" accommodation offered to poor emigrants making the long trek across the Atlantic in the late 1800's. This was no great discomfort to the navvies, however, as they only used the Caiplie Hut for sleeping. Most of their spare time was spent in the local drinking establishments.

In an attempt to speed up construction of the line in the early months of 1883, the navvies were offered an increased hourly rate. The effect this had on the lifestyle of the workmen, however, was merely to increase their already high alcohol consumption. The men were paid fortnightly and every second Saturday night in Anstruther had been anything but peaceful ever since the workmen had taken up residence in the area.

Almost as soon as the navvies were paid, they made their way into town to the nearest "Dram Shop", with the result that every other weekend the local Police Cell was occupied with drunken employees of the railway contractor. One such drinking spree, in the Freemasons Hotel in Shore Street, Anstruther, on Saturday 5th May 1883, resulted in the death of a navvy, Joseph Robins.

Joseph had started drinking with some of his companions during the morning. By the time the hotel closed for the night, the group were so drunk that the barman decided to leave them where they were and go off to bed. Sometime later that night Joseph Robins fell over, and in doing so caught the collar of his shirt on a brass knob on the fireplace. His friends were in such a state of intoxication that they didn't see the unfortunate Joseph's predicament and the poor man was strangled to death.

So grief stricken were his drinking companions on learning of the death of their friend, that they set out from their bothy the next day in search of more alcohol with which to drown their sorrows. This they found at St Monance, where one of the party proceeded to join his recently deceased companion by drinking himself to death!

The main station building at Crail, opened in 1883 along with the first section of the Anstruther and St Andrews Railway (Author's collection).

By this time, work on the line was progressing rapidly, despite the drinking habits of the workers and, on Wednesday 2nd May 1883, the line was opened between Anstruther and Crail. It had not been the intention of the railway company to open the line until the summer, but demand from local farmers who wished to overcome "the weary and tedious journey to Anstruther" was such that a limited goods service was introduced.

The first train to work the line consisted of four wagons pulled by the Directors' own traction engine as far as Anstruther, where it was attached to the "Ordinary Special". The first three wagons contained "some twenty one prime oxen", whilst the fourth carried malt from a local brewery.

Demand for the services of the new railway were so great in the first few weeks of operation that a larger engine, described as being "a big iron horse in harness able to draw over eighty tons", was brought into service towards the end of the month.

At the beginning of June, work on the ballasting beyond Crail was reported to be progressing "at a rate of three hundred cubic yards per day" and "finishing touches" were being made to the station buildings along the line.

Kingsbarns station was closed to passengers in 1930, although the buildings remained intact until the line finally closed in 1965 (J. L. Stevenson).

On September 1st 1883, almost twenty tears to the day after the sound of the railway engine had first been heard in the East Neuk, the Anstruther and St Andrews Railway was opened to passengers between Anstruther and Boarhills. Crowds of spectators lined the platforms and the Dreel Viaduct from as early as six in the morning and, throughout the course of the day, many curious locals boarded the trains to visit the other stations on the new line.

The heavy rain that fell during the afternoon could do little to dampen the enthusiasm of the first day's passengers, who disembarked on their return to Anstruther "expressing delight over the experiences of the journey". The new station at Anstruther, however, was not quite ready for passenger use on that first day, which meant that for three months after the railway was opened to Boarhills, passenger trains had to reverse into the original terminus.

B1 No.61118 coasts through Boarhills station heading towards Kingsbarns on August 21st 1956 (A.G. Ellis Collection).

Having to utilise the original station also raised a problem whereby there was no facility in place for the engine to run around the carriages in order to be coupled with the opposite end of the train for the return journey. The only solution to this problem was for all trains departing from Anstruther and heading towards Crail to proceed firstly to Pittenweem, where the engine could run around the carriages and so be at the head of the train for the journey to Boarhills.

Until the line could be completed from Boarhills to St Andrews, passengers had to board a 'bus to complete their journey between these two points. Construction of this final section of the line, however, was painfully slow.

The estimated cost of completing the entire line from Anstruther to St Andrews had now risen to £125,000 as compared with the figure of £56,000 quoted by the original contractor. This meant that work could not continue until a considerable amount of further capital had been raised.

It was to be November of 1884 before the company could announce that the purchase of land between Boarhills and St Andrews was complete, but by May of 1885 the Directors still needed a further £5,000 before the work could be put out to contract.

A mixture of LMS and Great Western wagons occupy the goods sidings at a tranquil MountMelville station (Lens of Sutton).

Eventually the required sum was realised and, by November 1885, the Chairman was happy to report that work had re-started and that great progress was being made. The contractor, announced the Chairman at a meeting of the shareholders, was "the right man in the right place at last".

Perhaps the right man had been found at last, but even the new contractor could do nothing about the severe winter of 1885-1886 that was to delay progress once again. Nor could anything be done about the unseasonable weather that was to follow in August 1886, or the severe frosts encountered in

December 1886 and January 1887. Slowly but surely, though, the line progressed towards St Andrews and in May 1887 the final link in the chain which was to become the "Fife Coast Line" was inspected by the Board of Trade. Particular attention was given to the inspection of the iron bridges on the line, no doubt the "usual severe test" being applied in the wake of the TayBridge disaster.

The Anstruther and St Andrews Railway was opened in its entirety on 1st June 1887 and initial passenger figures were such that Chairman John Purvis announced at the next shareholders meeting that he had come before them that day "with a more cheerful face than ever he had done at any previous meeting".

With the completion of the Fife Coast Line, the opening of the new TayBridge and the anticipated opening of the ForthBridge, a line of rails would soon exist around the coast of Fife between Dundee and Edinburgh. This exciting prospect resulted in many ideas being put forward to the railway companies by the people of the East Neuk villages.

Some people wanted to see the introduction of a cheap single fare that would enable them to visit Dundee, or indeed Edinburgh for that matter. Such tickets were available from St Andrews, so why not from Anstruther? Others wanted special excursion trains to be put on for the same reasons.

Another idea came from Kilrenny Town Council, who decided to petition the North British Railway with a view to running an express service between Dundee and Edinburgh via the Fife coast, with the only stops being at Crail, Anstruther and Elie during its entire journey. This proposal was supported by Crail Town Council, who also petitioned the North British Railway Company.

Before long, the coast burghs had become so accessible due to the vast improvement in railway communications, that they soon became a popular destination for visitors from all walks of life. By the late 1880's, Crail was being visited by artists, historians, photographers and crowds of tourists, flocking to the town to bathe in the cold waters of the Forth estuary.

The village of Crail lay almost undiscovered until the opening of the railway in 1883 made it a popular destination for artists, photographers and tourists (Author's collection).

The Anstruther and St Andrews Railway Company was not, however, taken over during its very early days of operation by the North British Railway as had been anticipated. The Anstruther and St Andrews continued to exist as an independent concern almost until the end of the century; the North British Railway Company eventually gaining control of the entire line around the east coast of Fife in 1897.

One suspects that the resistance to any sort of takeover during these first years of operation was a throwback to the uncertainty that had existed between the two companies when agreement to form a junction between the two railways was sought in the 1880's!

Chapter Eight
THE TWENTIETH CENTURY

St Andrews Station was situated in a cutting, with the main station building located on an island platform (Lens of Sutton).

The new century dawned and the Fife Coast Line, as the entire railway round the coast from Thornton to Leuchars had become affectionately known by this time, entered the period that many people regard as being the "golden age" of Britain's railways. Rail travel was at this time becoming increasingly popular in the Fife peninsula, with timetables published at the turn of the century showing significant increases from the corresponding timetables of the mid to late 1800's.

The century was still in its infancy, however, when in July 1901 the station at St Andrews was almost completely destroyed by fire. The blaze was discovered just after midnight on July 3rd and, although the local Fire Brigade were quickly on the scene, little could be done to save the main station building. A report in the "Dundee Courier" the following day described the aftermath:

"Of the main building nothing remains except the iron beams and the pillars and some masonry work. The staircase leading to the platform and the bookstall was saved".

The report goes on to say that this had been the second fire at the station in the space of five days.

Passenger traffic continued to rise in the years leading up to the First World War and, in 1910, the amount of visitors to the East Neuk burghs was such that an express service was inaugurated from Glasgow to Crail. Initially, the "Fifeshire Coast Express" ran daily throughout the summer months, the only stops being at Leven, Elie and Anstruther before terminating at Crail only two hours after leaving Glasgow.

Another service which ran between Edinburgh and the East Neuk of Fife at this time was a golfers' train, which operated on Saturday afternoons during the summer. This service was introduced in the late 1890's and called at all golfing towns situated on the southern coast of Fife, terminating at Crail.

Goods traffic also continued to rise during the early part of the century, with mineral traffic showing a marked increase just before the First World War between Thornton and Leven. The reason for the increase on this particular part of the line was due mainly to the opening in 1913 of the new No.3 dock at Methil, from where the export of coal had been rapidly increasing since the first dock was opened in 1887. The track between Thornton and Leven was doubled to cope with the increased amount of coal trains using the line and the Leven harbour branch, which by this time had been extended round to Methil, was quadrupled.

A large marshalling yard was built on the north bank of the River Leven, about a mile west of Leven station, to accommodate the increased number of coal wagons required to cope with the additional traffic.

Only a year and a half after the opening of the new dock, however, came the outbreak of the Great War in 1914 and, with it, the first mention of services on the Fife Coast Line being curtailed, when it was proposed to close Pittenweem station as a direct result of the manpower shortage brought about by the conflict. As one would expect, this was met with much protest from the Town Council and from the people of Pittenweem.

A number of cases were presented to the railway company and to the Board of Trade in a vain attempt to reopen the station. In February 1917, a delegation from Pittenweem Town Council met with Mr Asquith, M.P. and drew his attention to an agreement made in 1861 between the East of Fife Railway Company and the Town Council. This agreement stated that one of the conditions relating to the purchase of certain lands from the Town Council during the construction of the line was that all ordinary trains would stop at Pittenweem. The delegation also made the point that the manpower required to keep the station open was less than that which was now required to cart goods between Anstruther and Pittenweem and vice versa.

The wishes of the Council were partly granted when on 14th March, 1917, the station was reopened for goods traffic only. The Council continued their campaign to have a passenger service re-instated, but despite further protests, the Board of Trade would not reverse their decision.

The townsfolk of Pittenweem were therefore resigned to having to find their way to Anstruther or St Monance to use the train service for the remainder of the war. To everyone's relief, the station was fully reopened shortly after the hostilities ended, with the passenger trains once again stopping at Pittenweem from February 1st 1919.

Pittenweem station during the early part of the twentieth century. The station was closed for most of the First World War due to a manpower shortage, eventually re-opening in February 1919 (Author's collection).

The end of the Great War also saw the resurrection of the Fife coast towns and villages as tourist resorts. In addition to the original express service that had been instated between Glasgow and Crail before the war, a second "Fifeshire Coast Express" was added to the timetable, this time running between Edinburgh and Crail.

The two trains did not, however, complete the journey independent of one another. On reaching Dalmeny, on the southern end of the Forth Bridge, the coaches from the Glasgow express were coupled on to the Edinburgh train, and the two expresses completed the journey as one unit.

A restaurant car was also added to the service around this time, forming part of the Edinburgh train, but was withdrawn in 1920. Incidentally, this was the same year that saw the opening of the station bookstall at Anstruther.

The most significant change to occur during the years between the wars was the "grouping" of the railway companies to form

"The Big Four", namely the London and North Eastern, the London Midland and Scottish, the Great Western and the Southern Railway Companies.

The North British Railway, who had controlled the Fife Coast Line since the late 1800's, became part of the London and North Eastern Railway on New Year's Day 1923, under the North Eastern, Eastern and East Scottish Group Amalgamation Scheme 1922.

In the autumn of 1930 the four intermediate stations between Crail and St Andrews all lost their passenger status. Kingsbarns, Boarhills, Stravithie and MountMelville had never enjoyed the same passenger traffic as the other stations on the line had done and few, if any, were surprised when the decision was made. Goods traffic continued to be handled, but this too had been in decline in the years following the First World War.

In 1939, the country was once again plunged into a World War and once again railway services were curtailed. When hostilities eventually ceased in 1945, the express service from Glasgow was re-introduced during the summer months for the anticipated heavy influx of holidaymakers from the west.

The new "Fife Coast Express" called at Burntisland, Kirkcaldy, Leven, Elie, Anstruther, Crail and, unlike its predecessor, continued on to St Andrews, completing the journey in three hours. Passengers on the new service had the added comfort of travelling in carriages inherited from the "Silver Jubilee" express, which was a prestigious express service introduced in 1935 to connect London with Newcastle.

Another event brought about by the end of the Second World War was nationalisation and the formation of British Railways. The amalgamation of the "Big Four" group of railway companies into one had first been discussed during the early years of the war.

The 'FifeCoast Express' hauled by Thomson B1 N0.61172 departs from Crail bound for St Andrews on August 22nd 1956 (A.G. Ellis Collection).

With the election of a Labour Government in 1945, it was clear that a nationalised railway system was not far away and this inevitability became reality on 1st January 1948. The green livery of the LNER engines would never be seen again in the East of Fife.

In those days before the motor car became an accepted part of family life, the train was seen as being a vital link between the small towns and villages and the larger cities. Two or perhaps three times per year, families from the East Neuk towns would board the trains to travel to Dundee or Edinburgh with the intention of purchasing some merchandise that could not be bought locally. These shopping trips were an event which was looked forward to and families would always don their "best claes" for the occasion.

One former resident of the East Neuk recalls an amusing incident connected with such an excursion, when he and his family were waiting on a train at Waverley station in Edinburgh at the end of a day's shopping. As the train drew into the platform, the message came over the loudspeaker system that their train was bound for Dundee and would be calling at Dalmeny, North Queensferry, Inverkeithing, Aberdour, Burntisland, Kinghorn, Kirkcaldy, Kirkcaldy Sinclairtown, Dysart, Thornton, Cameron Bridge, Leven, Lundin Links, Largo, Kilconquhar, Elie, St Monance, Pittenweem, Anstruther, Crail, St Andrews, Leuchars and Dundee. The announcement seemed to go on for ever, and the passengers assembled on the platform burst into a round of applause in recognition of the breathless announcers' achievement when the last station was finally declared!

Another amusing story connected with the "occasion" of a trip to Edinburgh is recalled by one passenger who witnessed an elderly lady attempting to alight from a train at St Monance station fully laden with her day's shopping. Seeing that the tired and weary shopper was encountering some considerable difficulty in doing so, a smartly dressed and well spoken gentleman offered to lend a hand with her parcels.
When the struggling passenger and her shopping were successfully disembarked, the woman thanked the gentleman for his kind assistance. "Don't mention it" said the gent, stepping back on to the train. "Wha me? Ah'll no tell a sowell" came the reply!

The motor car, though, continued to increase in popularity and the days of the shopping trips by train were numbered and, as the number of families owning cars increased, passenger figures slumped. By the mid 1960's, passenger timetables showed that the frequency of trains travelling daily in each direction had almost fallen to the amount which had been published in the timetables of the late 1850's, when the line was first opened.

As for goods traffic, this too started to go into decline after the Second World War. The herring fishing, which had for so long been the main source of employment in the East Neuk of Fife, all but disappeared from the Forth in the late 1940's and with it went a major source of revenue for the railway.

67

Never again would Anstruther Town Council have to appeal to the railway company for assistance in repairing the road between the harbour and the station.

Fishing in the East Neuk after the decline of the herring industry was largely centred on the white fish industry, with the local fleet operating mainly from Pittenweem. With Pittenweem fish market being almost a mile by road from the station and with road transport becoming increasingly popular as roads and vehicles were improved, fish traffic on the Fife Coast Line became almost non existent by the 1960's. The days when the newspapers reported that there was insufficient railway wagons at Anstruther station to cope with the fish being carted up from the harbour would never be seen again.

With the movement of farm produce and minerals also giving way to transportation by road, all railway goods traffic both in and out of the East Neuk had fallen to insignificant levels by the time the decision was taken to close the line. When Doctor Beeching scythed his way through Britain's branch lines in the mid 1960's, there could be little hope for a railway that served an area of little industrial significance.

The only hope that anyone had of the line remaining open in its entirety lay in the tourist industry, but even an appeal on this basis could not grant a stay of execution for the East Neuk.

Anstruther harbour during the halcyon days of the herring fishing industry. Always a great source of revenue for the railway company, the industry rapidly went into decline shortly after the Second World War (Author's Collection).

Thomson Class B1 No. 61132 departs from Crail in 1965, the last year of scheduled passenger services in the East Neuk of Fife.

(Author's Collection)

Chapter Nine
AROUND THE EASTCOAST OF FIFE

A Crail-bound Diesel Multiple Unit waits to depart from Thornton Junction in September 1959 (Mrs Shirley Corstorphine).

Any intending passenger waiting for a train at Thornton Junction station during the 1950's or 1960's could not fail to notice the subsidence that affected both station platforms and buildings, caused by the mine workings of the nearby Balgonie Pit.

The main reason for this was that during the early part of the twentieth century, the pit mine workings had started to encroach on the station. Realising that any further encroachment would cause their land to become unstable, the railway company asked the coal company not to mine beneath the station.

The coal company, however, demanded £96,000 in compensation for complying with the request. The railway company refused to pay up, the coal was subsequently removed from beneath the station and the station began to subside, initiating years of worry for the railway company.

As the station sank, the platforms had to be built up and the original sandstone station buildings were replaced by lighter wooden ones. The demolition of the original buildings was itself something of a tragedy, as they were, by all accounts, grand structures. One former railway employee recalls this once proud station as having first and third class waiting rooms and a refreshment bar, with polished interior woodwork and swing doors with "refreshment rooms" painted on the glass.

The subsidence was so bad that the platforms of 1910 were actually below the rail level by the 1960's. A gang of workmen were constantly employed on the duty of ballasting the rails to the correct level, as the track sank appreciably every day. Some even estimated that the rails and platforms had been built up some fourteen to fifteen feet during this fifty year period. Eventually even the wooden buildings were deemed unsafe and by the early 1960's most of these had been abandoned.

The mine workings below the station were so near to the surface that the miners could hear the trains passing above them. Rumour has it that some miners even set their watches by the rumble of the 5am express!

This once busy rail junction, which at one time had employed two inspectors, thirteen porters and eight ticket collectors, was by the time of closure in 1969 little more than a quiet country station.

From Thornton, the Fife Coast Line branched off from the main line just to the north of the station and headed east towards CameronBridge. The line was double between this point and Leven and for almost the entire three miles from this point to CameronBridge station, the line took a course alongside the River Ore; first on the north bank, then crossed over to the south bank near to Wemyss Wood. Just after passing the point at which the rivers Ore and Leven merge, the line passed Cameron Bridge Distillery before entering the station.

It is rumoured that miners working just below the surface at Thornton Junction station used to set their watches by the rumble of the express trains passing overhead! (Mrs Shirley Corstorphine).

CameronBridge station was situated at the southern end of the village of Windygates and was almost entirely surrounded by the distillery. The main station building, which was a small wooden construction completely surrounded by a canopy, was situated on an island platform. Access to the platform was gained by using the steps down from the road bridge at the eastern end of the station. The only other building on the passenger platform was a store constructed from corrugated iron, which was situated to the west of the main building.

A lattice footbridge crossed the western end of the station, but it provided no access to the passenger platform. The purpose of this bridge was merely to maintain a right of way through the station site. To the west of the footbridge there existed a signal box, at the point where the extensive distillery rail network branched off. Goods platforms were situated both to the north and south of the main platform. At one time, a mineral line leading to Buckhaven also branched off to the south of the station.

Heading east from CameronBridge, the line ran along the north bank of the River Leven for a distance of just over a mile before reaching the East Fife Central Junction and signal box. This junction was where the East Fife Central Railway branched off and headed north towards Kennoway. This railway, opened in 1898, was reputed to be the longest "goods only" railway in the country, serving the villages and farming communities of Kennoway, Montrave and Largoward before terminating at Lochty.

Just after passing East Fife Central Junction, the line passed to the north of the National Steel Foundry, served by a private siding which branched off to the south across the river. To the east of this point a footbridge crossed the line and marked the western end of Kirkland Goods Yard.

Kirkland Yard was constructed in 1912 to accommodate the additional wagons required to convey the coal traffic generated by the opening of the No.3 dock at Methil. The line serving Methil Docks and the Shorehead sidings at Leven branched off from the south eastern end of the yard.

Leaving the east end of Kirkland Yard, the line ran parallel with Leven's Montgomery Drive before passing through Leven goods station, which was the original passenger terminus of the Leven Railway. The goods station consisted of a cluster of small sidings surrounding a single platform and was situated where the small group of industrial units now exists at Burnmill Road.

After passing under Glenlyon Road, the line entered Leven station, which was situated where the houses at Station Court now exist. This station superseded the original station in 1885. Platforms and station buildings existed on both sides of the track, with a signal box situated on the south platform, to the east of the main station building.

Departing from Leven station, the line passed along the south side of Rose Terrace before crossing Waggon Road by way of a level crossing, then continued east between Haughgate Terrace and Lemon Terrace before passing under Scoonie Road. A small siding once existed at this point to serve the Cuttlehill Brick and Tile works, the site of which was later occupied by Deas the Baker.

After passing under Scoonie Road, the line passed alongside Balmoral Terrace before reaching Scoonie Burn. It was at this point that the double track ended and from here round the coast to Leuchars the line was single; the only double track being at stations or passing loops.

The obvious danger that exists with single track railways is the possibility that two trains travelling in opposite directions could meet head on. On the Fife Coast Line and indeed on most other single track railways in Britain, this problem was overcome by using the "electric tablet" system.

The principle behind this system was that the entire line was divided into sections, with each section having a tablet assigned to it. Before a train could proceed onto a single track system, the driver would have to be in possession of the tablet assigned to the section of single track he was entering, which would be obtained from the signal box at the start of the section. To speed up the system, the tablets were often exchanged as the engine was still moving and for this purpose, small platforms called "tablet catchers" were installed at the start of each section for the signalman to stand on.

This system did throw up one particular problem, however. If the driver of an engine entering a section of single track took the tablet for that section on to the next signal box, how could a train following on behind enter the section without the tablet first being returned to the signalman at the start of the section?

This problem was overcome by using a system where each section of track had not one, but several tablets assigned to it. The signal boxes at either end of the section contained machines into which the tablets were installed, with the machines in each box being interconnected so as to allow the removal of only one tablet at any one time. The tablet for the section of track now being described would have been obtained at Leven station.

The tablet catching platform at Kingsbarns (A.G. Ellis Collection).

After passing through a small cutting to the rear of East Links, the line then headed out over the Leven Links golf course. At this point, a siding owned by the Fife Coal Company once branched off to the north to serve the Durie Pit, which was situated to the north of the raised ground locals know today as "The Bing".

The line then ran across the golf course, passing to the south of Silverburn, where a siding branched off near to the "Mile

Dyke" to serve the Silverburn Flax Mill, which was operated by Tullis Russell Ltd. This was one of the first sidings on the East of Fife Railway and existed until the 1950's.

Lundin Links golf course was then crossed before arriving at Lundin Links station, which was situated at the edge of the course on Station Road to the rear of the Old Manor Hotel. The track was single as it passed through the station and a small goods siding with loading platform branched off to the north. The only passenger platform at Lundin Links was located on the north side of the track, where a wooden waiting room with canopy was located alongside the main station building.

Leaving the station, the line continued east over Golf Road before passing the golf clubhouse, then passed under Drummochy Road. At this point the climb began toward the viaduct over the Keil Burn and Largo station. The viaduct still exists, but there is now no trace of the station.

The track doubled as it passed through the station, which had the main station building and signal box situated on the south platform. A lattice footbridge served the north platform, where there was a small waiting room. A goods yard was situated on the north side of the station.

Departing from Largo the line passed to the north of the TempleCottages and continued eastwards towards Dumbarnie Links. Just before reaching Dumbarnie, at a point midway between "Viewforth House" and "Carrick Villa", there existed in the 1920's a siding which branched off to the south and ran on to the beach. This was known as the Strathairlie siding and was operated by the McAlpine Construction Company. There was a lot of construction work in Fife at this time and the sand from Dumbarnie was used for building purposes.

Continuing eastwards, the railway traversed open countryside and started to head inland, keeping a fairly straight and level course. About a mile to the west of Kilconquhar station, there existed a passing loop and signal box.

Kilconquhar station was the original terminus of the East of Fife Railway when it was first opened in 1857. It was located at the junction of the A917 Largo to Elie road and the private road which leads to ShellBay. The only passenger platform was situated on the north side of the track, which was double at this point, along with the station building and Station Master's house. There was a small goods yard and loading platform to the south of the main track. Some of the platforms at Kilconquhar still exist, as well as one of the station buildings which has now been converted into a private residence.

A lone passenger waiting on an east-bound train enjoys the pleasant afternoon sunshine at Elie on 21st August 1956 (A.G. Ellis Collection).

On leaving Kilconquhar, the line turned to the right and headed in a south easterly direction, before entering Elie by passing under the A917 just to the north of the primary school. It then passed through a cutting alongside Woodside Road, and then passed under the A917 again before entering Elie station, which was situated where the new bungalows at Baird Place were later built.

The line was double as it passed through the station and there were passenger platforms and station buildings on both sides of the track, connected by a footbridge. A small goods yard lay to the south of the station.

Class 37 No.64618 pulling a mixed train is about to pass under the 'Waterless Brig' between Pittenweem and St Monance (Author's Collection).

Leaving Elie, the line took a route between the sea and the main road. The railway between Elie and St Monance was perhaps the most scenic part of the route, with uninterrupted views of the MayIsland and the Bass Rock to be had to the south as the line passed alongside Ardross beach. The ruined NewarkCastle, which stands on the top of a cliff just to the west of St Monance, could be seen shortly before reaching St Monance station.

St Monance station was situated on the north western edge of the town, where there now exists a small industrial estate. There were passenger platforms on both sides of the track, which doubled on entering the station. The main station building and signal box were situated on the north platform.

A lattice footbridge connected the north and south platforms, and also spanned the entrance to the goods yard, which lay to the south of the passenger station, to provide pedestrian access from Queen Margaret Street.Passing under the A917 once more on leaving St Monance, the line headed away from the coast through open farmland before passing under the B942 by way of the road bridge known to locals as the "Waterless Brig".

The next stop after St Monance was Pittenweem. This station was situated on the minor road between Pittenweem and Ovenstone, about half a mile to the north of the village. There was only one passenger platform, although the line doubled on entering the station. A small goods yard was located to the south.

The mile or so of track east of Pittenweem, which separated that station from Anstruther, was fairly straight and level and was bounded on both sides by farmland.

Anstruther West signal box and the bridge carrying the minor road connecting Easter Grangemuir and Crawhill farms with West Anstruther marked the start of Anstruther goods yard. The line doubled on passing the signal box and the extensive goods station branched off to the south at this point.

Anstruther goods station was originally the passenger terminus of the East of Fife Railway after the line was extended from Kilconquhar in 1863. The later passenger station was built on the opposite side of the viaduct spanning the Dreel Burn in 1883, when the Anstruther and St Andrews Railway opened as far as Boarhills.

The goods station was the largest of any of the East Neuk stations and boasted a turntable, which was situated immediately to the west of the Dreel Viaduct. There was also an engine shed and goods shed. The original passenger station buildings which formed part of the goods station survived intact until final closure of the line in the 1960's, although they had been out of use for over eighty years!

The later passenger station, on the opposite side of the Dreel Viaduct, consisted of passenger platforms on either side of the line connected by a footbridge. The main station building was situated on the south platform and on the north platform there was a small waiting room. There was also at one time a signal box to the east of this point, which was demolished when the points were removed from the eastern end of the station.

Leaving Anstruther and heading towards Crail, the track passed alongside the WaidAcademy, with its rugby and hockey pitches. Pupils from the WaidAcademy used the train daily to get to and from school, as the school's catchment area spanned all of the East Neuk villages from Kilconquhar to Crail.

From here, the line headed away from the coast and passed to the north of the village of Kilrenny, passing through the woods known to local boys as "Little Africa". The line then continued to head inland for a short distance before heading back towards the sea and running alongside the A917 coast road once more just before reaching Crail.

The station at Crail was situated on the north side of the village. It was a fairly busy station during the summer months and was noted for its floral displays, as were most of the village stations on the line. It is perhaps fitting, therefore, that the station site now finds itself in use as a garden centre!

The main station building was sited on the east platform, from where a lattice footbridge spanned the double track to connect with the west platform, on which there was a small wooden waiting room. At the northern end of the east platform there was a signal box, which marked the entrance to the goods yard which lay behind the main station building.

Leaving Crail, the line continued northwards, keeping a fairly straight and level course through open farmland before reaching Kingsbarns, where there was a passing loop and signal box. This station was situated on the minor road heading west from Kingsbarns towards North Quarter Farm. Kingsbarns station, along with Boarhills, Stravithie and Mount Melville, the next three stations on the route, were closed to passengers in the 1930's although their small goods yards remained open for the occasional goods traffic. The passing loop and signal box at Kingsbarns remained operational until final closure of the line.

Crail station, looking north towards Kingsbarns (Lens of Sutton).

Continuing in a northerly direction from Kingsbarns, the next stop was Boarhills, whose station lay to the south of the village at the northern end of the viaduct which spanned the Kenly Water. A small goods yard branched off to the north and lay alongside the main A917 Crail to St Andrews road. At Boarhills, the line turned to head towards Stravithie which lay two miles to the west across open countryside.

Stravithie station occupied a position immediately to the east of the B9131 Anstruther to St Andrews road. The track bed at

Stravithie was wide enough to accommodate a double track and had platforms on both sides of the line, although only one track was ever laid.

One possible reason for this double track bed was to accommodate a junction with an extension of the East Fife Central Railway, the goods line which ran between CameronBridge and Lochty. There is evidence that Stravithie was being considered as the terminus of the East Fife Central Railway when the line was first proposed in the late nineteenth century.

The double track bed and platforms at Stravithie (A.G. Ellis Collection).

Another possible explanation for the double track bed is that allowance had been made for the future installation of a passing loop somewhere between St Andrews and Kingsbarns. As Stravithie was situated almost exactly equidistant between the two, it would have been an ideal location.

The only station building at Stravithie was situated on the south platform, and the only other feature was a small goods yard which branched off to the south as the line entered the east end of the station.

The next station was MountMelville, which lay about two and a half miles to the west of Stravithie through open farmland. This station was located amongst a clump of trees alongside the A915 Largo to St Andrews road and consisted of a single platform and station building on the north side of the track, with a small goods yard branching off to the south.

Although they had been out of use for several years, the buildings at all four rural stations between Crail and St Andrews; Kingsbarns, Boarhills, Stravithie and Mount Melville; remained intact until Doctor Beeching's axe fell. The station building at Stravithie escaped demolition and now forms part of a guest house which has been rather appropriately named "The Old Station". The owners of the guest house have even installed an old railway carriage where the track bed was once situated, which now houses luxury suite accommodation!

From MountMelville, the line turned sharply north, passing Cairnsmill Farm before taking a large sweeping curve to head north east as it began to descend into St Andrews, approaching the town from the south. The railway entered St Andrews by running alongside Largo Road, then passing behind Sloan Street and Wallace Street before crossing over the Kinness Burn Viaduct. The final approach to the station was made by passing under Argyle Street and Doubledykes Road.

St Andrews station lay in a cutting adjacent to the 'bus station on City Road. The station building was located under a large canopy on an island platform, access to which could be had by using footbridges from either side of the station, although the main entrance was from the 'bus station. The track split to run round the island platform on entering the station and remained doubled for a short distance after leaving the station to the north. A small siding branched off to the east, behind the 'bus garage.

One of the most noticeable features of St Andrews station in the summer months was the baskets of flowers which were suspended from the canopy and the flower pots which were placed along the embankments. The station staff took great pride in their floral displays and, according to former Station Master Mr J.M.Bennet, the station won many prestigious awards over the years in the Station Gardens Competition.

St Andrews goods station was situated about half a mile to the north-west of the passenger station, on the other side of the bridge crossing Pilmour Links, and was located alongside the famous golf course where the game was first played in 1754. This was the original passenger station and terminus of the St Andrews Railway when it was first opened from Leuchars in 1852.

The goods station consisted of an array of sidings, around which were placed an engine shed, a goods shed, a coal yard, offices and the Station Master's house. The coal sheds were actually a recognised feature of the famous Old Course and many a golfer would attempt to clear the sheds with a direct shot, rather than play around them! At the north end of the goods station was the Links signal box, which afforded the signalmen a grandstand view of both the Old and Eden golf courses. When the line was finally closed in 1969, the site of the goods station was built over by the Old Course Hotel.

Leaving St Andrews to the north-west, the line crossed over the golf links, then ran alongside the estuary of the River Eden before eventually crossing the river at Guardbridge just after passing behind the reputedly haunted Guardbridge Hotel.

Guardbridge station was situated at the west end of the bridge, alongside the A919 road connecting Guardbridge with Leuchars, which was negotiated by level crossing. There was only one passenger platform at Guardbridge, which was situated on the north side of the track. Goods sidings, loading platforms and a crane lay to the south, as well as a signal box which was sited alongside the level crossing.

On leaving the station, the line turned sharply north, running behind the houses on Main Street before passing the exchange sidings serving Guardbridge Paper Mill. The paper mill generated a considerable amount of rail traffic and had its own internal rail system, which was worked by a battery powered shunting engine. For fire safety reasons, conventionally powered engines could not be used within the confines of the mill as a spark from a steam engine could obviously cause untold damage!

From here, the line curved round to the west before crossing Motray Water. A few hundred yards farther on the Fife Coast Line ended by re-joining the main Edinburgh to Dundee line at Milton, shortly before entering Leuchars Junction station.

Chapter Ten
THE BEECHING CUTS

A busy scene at St Monance during the 1960's. Thomson class B1 No.61103 heads east towards Pittenweem, whilst a mineral train with engines at both ends waits beside the south platform. (C.W.R. Bowman).

The section of the Fife Coast Line from Leven round the coast to St Andrews was closed to passengers, along with Guardbridge station, in September 1965. Many rural areas lost their train service during the early to mid 1960's, due to the cuts imposed by Dr Richard (later Lord) Beeching, Chairman of the British Railways Board established under the Conservative Government's 1963 Transport Act.

Cuts in rail services in the eastern part of the county had first been implemented in 1930 with the closure of the four intermediate stations between Crail and St Andrews. The closure of the passenger stations at Kingsbarns, Boarhills, Stravithie and MountMelville would appear to have passed off with little protest from the communities which they served, which was hardly surprising considering the location of the stations concerned.

Declining passenger and goods traffic in the late 1950's and early 1960's once again brought about the question of curtailment of train services around the East Neuk of Fife and, when British Railways announced their intention to close the line between Leven and St Andrews in the early 1960's, the proposals were greeted with much anger and protest by the local people.

In October 1963 Provost Braid of St Monance and Provost Scott of Elie were appointed official representatives of the East Neuk of Fife in the fight to save the line and, as such, urged that "every possible protest should be lodged by the people living between St Andrews and Leven".

In a series of meetings held between 1963 and 1965, Provost Braid was most vociferous in his attempts to make the railway authorities think again. In February 1964 he claimed that all the good work that had been done by the local authorities to boost their burghs as tourist attractions would be undone by closing the East Neuk railway to passengers. He also pointed out that amongst the people who would suffer as a result of closure were around 100 pupils of the WaidAcademy who used the railway to get to and from school. Provost Braid's fears for the tourist industry were backed up by Fife County Council and Tourist Board, who stated that the main industry in the East Neuk was now tourism and it was therefore essential that rail services be maintained.

Mr Ron Prime, manager of the holiday camp in Cellardyke, stated that during his twelve week season, 3,500 holidaymakers using the camp came to Anstruther by train. "They really bring all the house" he said. "I doubt if they could ever get their luggage on a bus".

The arguments raged on and in August 1965 at a meeting between representatives of the East Neuk burghs and British

Rail held in Glasgow, Sir John Gilmour, Member of Parliament for East Fife, said that British Rail had authorised closure on the grounds that adequate alternative public transport would be available to connect the east coast burghs with Leven station, which would remain open as the railhead for the east of Fife. Sir John was adamant that these alternative arrangements were inadequate and, as a result of poor bus connections and parking, it was his opinion that Leven station would also be facing closure in a couple of years. How right he was!

Alas, the protests fell on deaf ears, and British Rail announced their intention to proceed with closure. Provost James Braid refused to be defeated, however, and announced an ambitious plan to keep the line open. His proposal was that by using two diesel trains and four crews, four trains per day could travel between Dundee and Edinburgh via the coast. Some of the stations on the line could become unmanned halts and the level crossings could be converted to automatic working. British Railways refused to listen and duly announced that under the terms of the Transport Act of 1962, all railway passenger train services between Leven and St Andrews via Anstruther would be withdrawn on and from Monday 6th September 1965.

The last train to travel on the St Andrews to Leven section of the Fife Coast Line was the early evening service from Crail bound for Glasgow on Sunday 5th September 1965, although the last train to travel the entire route between Leven and St Andrews had made the journey late the previous evening.

Crowds gathered at Crail to witness the departure of the last train. Demand for tickets by those wishing to be one of the last to travel the route was so great that the ticket office actually ran out and were forced to issue return tickets to satisfy the intending travellers! It was a sentimental journey for many of the passengers, including a number of former railway employees from Thornton who had worked on the line. One retired engine driver who made the trip expressed his disappointment not only that the line was to close, but that British Rail hadn't put on a "real" train for the last run.

A deputation from St Monance Town Council, including Provost James Braid, also made the journey. Even at this late stage, the Provost didn't think that this would be the last passenger train to use the line, stating that the Provosts of the five East Neuk burghs were still looking into the possibility that the line could be bought from British Rail along with an old locomotive and run as a community effort. Alas it was not to be.

At precisely 18:07, driver Jimmy Dobson of Glasgow sounded the horn and the last train from Crail pulled out of the station. All along the line the diesel was greeted by emotional scenes. Detonators were placed on the line at Pittenweem and crowds gathered at every station between Crail and Leven to witness the end of an era.

When the train finally pulled into Leven, the porter who was waiting to collect the last "tablet" from the line had it handed to him attached to a yellow balloon. As the passengers disembarked, one girl sent driver Dobson on his way with a kiss on the cheek. Slowly the crowd dispersed and the passengers from the East Neuk boarded a coach specially laid on for the sad journey home.

The line east of Leven remained open to goods traffic, but inevitably this too ceased just one year later. British Railways then wasted no time in lifting the track, and any remote chance that there may have been of re-opening the East of Fife Railway was gone. Evidence that there ever was a railway around the East Neuk has now largely disappeared back into the landscape, but a few signs still remain, most notably the viaduct at Lower Largo. Restoration work carried out in 1993 has ensured that this well known landmark will be standing for some time to come.

Chapter Eleven
THE END OF THE LINE

No sooner had the line from Leven round the coast to St Andrews been severed, than the threat of closure once again reared it's ugly head, this time with reference to the passenger services to both Leven and St Andrews. Both railways had seen a decline in passenger use as a direct result of the Beeching cuts in 1965 and in the summer of 1967 British Railways announced its intention to close several passenger stations in Fife, including those at St Andrews, Thornton Junction, CameronBridge and Leven.

Lord Beeching had by this time departed the political scene and his Conservative Government had bowed out to a landslide Labour victory in 1966. In July 1967, St Andrews Town Council decided to write to the new Minister of Transport, Barbara Castle, to ask for closure of the station at St Andrews to be delayed at least until the forthcoming Tayside Development Plan was available for consultation.

The Council felt that St Andrews was very much a part of this plan and good commuter rail links with Dundee were vital. The prospect of having to endure a 48 minute bus journey as compared with the rail journey time of 25 minutes was not one which the Council felt would be relished by regular travellers to and from the city.

Others who were sure to suffer the effects of closure were the 430 boarders and 50 teachers attending St Leonards School. The school admitted girls from all parts of the United Kingdom and, if St Andrews station were to close, then the school would have to arrange for the pupils to be transported to and from Leuchars station by coach. University students would also have to find alternative means of transporting themselves and their considerable luggage between St Andrews and the main line. In addition, St Andrews Merchants Association claimed that their livelihood depended on the delivery of goods to St Andrews by rail.

News of the possible closure of both the St Andrews and Leven stations was greeted with much anger and dismay by the inhabitants of the East Neuk burghs, who had relied on both stations since their service had been withdrawn in 1965. The inhabitants of the East Neuk had felt much frustration and difficulty in using public transport since their railway had been taken away and this situation looked set to get worse when, in May 1968, the local bus company proposed to cease the bus connections to and from Leven station. The bus service and timetable had been altered in 1965 in an effort to keep the railway accessible to the people from the East Neuk. Public opinion was that if this arrangement were to be ceased, then British Rail would surely carry out their intentions as passenger numbers would be further reduced as a direct result.

The following month, Leven Town Council realised that the threat of closure was very real and set about trying to find ways to save the town's train service, but the local inhabitants saw the Council's efforts as being too little too late. One report in the local paper at the time criticised the Town Council for "not realising this danger two or three years ago", when, in the opinion of the newspaper, more support should have been given to the campaign to save the service between Leven and St Andrews.

The fears of the local people were realised when intending passengers arriving at Leven, CameronBridge, Thornton and St Andrews stations on Saturday, 31st August 1968, were greeted with posters announcing withdrawal of passenger services in January of the following year.

"I have seen this coming for a long time" said Sir John Gilmour, calling for the people of Leven to mount a campaign to save the service. "We won't allow our station to be closed without a fight!"

Leven Town Council reacted to the announcement by lodging an objection with the Transport Users Consultative Committee. Provost James Braid of St Monance, a seasoned campaigner in fighting railway closures, offered advice to Leven Town Council, and suggested certain cost cutting measures which the Council could put before British Rail. These included staff cuts by reducing managerial and supervisory positions and downgrading stations to become unmanned halts, with all trains on the line being diesel railcars with fare collecting crews. The Provost also suggested exploring the possibility of saving on locomotive requirements by running combined freight and passenger trains.

Local businesses and institutions also publicly aired their displeasure at the announcement. Amongst these was the golf club factory in Glenlyon Road, who used the passenger service for the transportation of their product to customers far and wide. Around 100 employees of Balfour's foundry would now have to find their way to work by alternative means, as would the staff of CameronBridge hospital. Visitors to the hospital would also be inconvenienced.

With the campaign to keep the line open gathering steam, British Railways duly announced that closure of the Leven line had been deferred to allow time for a public enquiry. It seemed as though there was still a glimmer of hope.

St Andrews station, though, was not granted the same stay of execution. The protest to the Transport Minister by the Town Council and the appeal by the delegation from Fife County Council had all been in vain. The official date for closure of the St Andrews Railway was to be Monday, 6th January, 1969.

Towards the end of the year, the National Union of Railwaymen launched a scathing attack on British Railways. It was the opinion of the Union that timetables had been deliberately re-arranged so as to make the prospect of rail travel unattractive. This would cause passenger figures to drop even further, making closure justified and easier to implement. One example of this was the re-timing of the arrival of the Leven train at Haymarket station in Edinburgh, where passengers travelling from Leven through to Glasgow found that they had missed their connection by three minutes. British Railways denied any such ploy and claimed that the Haymarket staff were under instruction to hold the Glasgow trains until the Leven trains had arrived.

The New Year dawned and the sound of the bells had barely died away when, at 22:30 on Saturday, 4th January 1969, the last passenger train departed from St Andrews. Most of the passengers who crowded onto the blue diesel multiple unit only intended travelling as far as Leuchars, where they could board the last train back up the line to St Andrews.

The journey which had taken the very first train on the St Andrews Railway fifteen minutes to complete over one hundred years earlier, took on this occasion almost half an hour. Five times during the five mile journey, the communication cord was pulled and the train shuddered to a halt. On each occasion the guard made his way through the crowded train only to be greeted by innocent faces who claimed to know nothing about the cord being pulled!

At 11:07 the last train departed Leuchars for St Andrews, where the passengers were greeted by groups of University students singing songs especially composed to commemorate the closure. Slowly the crowds made their way up the staircase leading from the island platform and dispersed into the night. The dark and empty train departed for Dundee and another nail in the coffin of the Fife Coast Line was hammered home.

There was still hope for Leven, however. On 15th January 1969, a public hearing was held in the town's Scoonie Hall, when local people were given an opportunity to voice their disapproval at the closure of the Leven Railway to passenger traffic.

Many reasons were put forward for saving the line. The County Council argued that Leven was a holiday resort and, as such, depended on good railway connections. The Council spokesman also made the point that Levenmouth was one of five Special Development Districts in Scotland. Two factory units had recently been built in the town and more would be built in the near future. It was important that a rail connection be maintained to the area to support this development status.

The hearing went on for over three hours, during which time the discussion ranged from the difficulties that would be encountered by commuters travelling to work in Edinburgh, to a complaint from one gentleman who said that he would be unable to read "The Scotsman" on a bus due to the restricted elbow room. He would therefore be forced to buy the "Daily Record" or the "Bulletin" in future!

Those who attended the meeting also heard the accusation that British Railways had betrayed the people of the East Neuk of Fife. It was stated that promises had been made when the line round the coast was closed that Leven would remain open as the rail head for the towns lying further east.

The British Railways spokesman who attended the meeting denied this claim.

"I can refute any suggestion that we gave any guarantees at the time of the closure of the east Fife branch line" he stated. "We cannot give such guarantees and we did not give them".

It was clear from the mood of the meeting that any further appeal would prove fruitless and, in due course, British Railways announced that passenger services would be withdrawn on Monday, 6th October. As the Sunday rail service had already been withdrawn, this meant that the last train to pull out of Leven station would be the 8:25 train on Saturday, 4th October, 1969.

A sizeable crowd braved the chilly autumn evening to see the departure of the last train and to witness the end of an era. As the train drew out of the station, camera flash bulbs briefly lit up the six carriages of the blue diesel multiple unit as it slowly departed on its sad journey. The noise of the diesel engine rose as the train gathered speed, echoed as the train passed under Glenlyon Road, then slowly died away as it headed towards CameronBridge.

Around a hundred people made the last trip, including three retired railwaymen who occupied the compartment at the very rear of the train. The three former North British Railway signalmen stared sadly out of the rear window at the sight of Leven station disappearing into the night.

Some only travelled as far as Thornton, where a cheering crowd greeted the train. Some travelled as far as Kirkcaldy and a few travelled a little further down the line, no doubt wishing to make the most of this last sentimental journey.

The last passengers had departed the Fife Coast Line.

Preserved Class 5 No.44871 'Sovereign' at Leven in September 1991 (Author's Collection).

*A DMU bound for Dundee (TayBridge) about to depart from
Anstruther during the 1960's (Author's Collection)*

Chapter Twelve
THE PRESENT AND THE FUTURE

The former passenger station at CameronBridge in April 1991, with the distillery shunter and C02 wagons in the background (Author's Collection).

After the Leven Railway was closed to passengers in 1969, the line was retained on a "goods only" basis to serve Cameron Bridge Distillery at Windygates, Methil Power Station, Methil Docks and, for a short time, the Redpath Dorman Long oil rig fabrication yard at Methil (later R.G.C. Offshore).

Unfortunately, all goods traffic has now ceased. Although the rails are still extant, the junction with the main line at Thornton has now been severed.

The goods-only line was utilised by the distillery company for the despatch of the famous whisky produced at Cameron Bridge, as well as the import of grain, but by the early 1980's both of these activities had been transferred to road. A by-product of the distillation process, C02 gas, was also exported by rail tanker from the distillery in more recent times.

The distillery owned a small blue diesel shunter which, until closure of the line, could be seen busily moving CO_2 wagons to and from the exchange sidings and the large CO_2 storage tank within the distillery site.

Methil Power Station, opened shortly before the Leven Railway was closed to passengers, had large quantities of coal slurry and other combustible material delivered by rail.

The power station was the main reason that the line had remained open for goods traffic, and its decommission in 2000 appeared to have been the final nail in the coffin for the Leven line.

Class 37 'The Lass of Ballochmyle' enters CameronBridge with empty coal wagons from Methil power station on 18th April 1994 (Author's Collection).

The power station, like the distillery, operated its own diesel shunters to take the full wagons of coal from the sidings within the power station site to be emptied at the base of a coal grab, from where the combustible material was transferred to the furnaces.

Methil Docks saw little rail traffic in the years leading up to final closure. The export of coal, which at one time was so great that three million tons were exported from the port annually, had by the mid 1970's ceased altogether. Until the mid 1980's, considerable rail traffic was generated by the transport of imported wood pulp from the docks, which was destined for use in paper making. A daily service saw open wagons of the imported material carried over the Leven Railway destined for paper mills as far away as FortWilliam. The sidings at the docks were also used for the storage of 'Railfreight' vans, but this too ceased in the late 1980's.

Class 20 No.20201 crosses the River Leven on its way back from Methil Docks with a consignment of 'Railfreight' wagons on 17th February 1984 (Author's Collection).

The oil rig fabrication yard at Methil, which was opened in the early 1970's, was for a short time connected to the rail network. A short branch line, which extended along the northern side of the docks, entered the yard at its eastern end. Steel and various other items used in the building of oil production platforms were carried over this section of the line until it too gave way to road transport by the end of the decade.

Over the years since the closure of the stations at CameronBridge and Leven, several proposals have been put

101

forward in an effort to re-introduce passenger rail services to Levenmouth. Most of these proposals have been centred on the construction of a new station at Leven behind the swimming pool and the re-opening of the station at CameronBridge, where the platforms of the former passenger station are still intact.

A more ambitious suggestion was also put forward several years ago which proposed not only the re-introduction of passenger trains to Leven, but continuing the service round as far as Methil. As well as utilising the former station at CameronBridge, several unmanned halts were included in the proposals and were to be built at strategic points on the existing line, including such places as Kirkland, Mountfleurie and Innerleven. This system would not only have re-introduced a rail link between Leven and Kirkcaldy, but would have established a fast and efficient internal rail system interconnecting communities within the Levenmouth area.

Early in 1984, a front page headline in the 'East Fife Mail' again reported that the Levenmouth area could see the re-introduction of a passenger train service. The possibility that such a service could be introduced "before the end of the century" had been detailed in a "Policy Charter" drawn up between Fife Regional Council and British Rail. The charter stated that a feasibility study was to be carried out looking at the possibility of improving rail access to the major communities in the region that were not connected to the passenger rail network.

Future Scottish First Minister Henry McLeish, a Local Councillor in the Levenmouth area at the time of the report, welcomed the charter, commenting: "There has been some pressure from the Levenmouth community to see if a rail link would be a realistic proposition".

Later that same year, newspaper headlines once again reported on the proposed rail link with renewed optimism.

The opening of new stations in other similar-sized Scottish towns was seen as an indication that such propositions could eventually become reality.

The visit to Fife by Scottish Secretary of State Malcolm Rifkind in 1987 once again caused the Levenmouth Rail Link question to be raised. During a tour of the Fife Free Press headquarters in Kirkcaldy, East Fife Mail editor Ian Paterson took the opportunity to raise the matter with the Scottish Secretary and was met with a most favourable response. Mr Rifkind commented that he would be willing to look at the proposition of a passenger rail link between Leven and Kirkcaldy and that any information on the proposals should be sent to him at the Scottish Office.

In September 1991, it was the turn of the Scottish Association of Public Transport (SAPT) to put forward proposals for the re-opening of the line, and this group were hopeful that a 'sprinter' service could be introduced within two years to connect the Levenmouth area directly with Edinburgh. Unfortunately, this campaign also failed to materialise.

The topic has been raised several times since this book was first published in 1995 and, on one occasion, MSP Tricia Marwick even argued the case for the re-instatement of passenger services to Leven at a debate in the Scottish Parliament as she waved a copy of "East of Thornton Junction" at the assembly!

Following yet another failed attempt to have the railway re-instated in 2008, the formation of the Levenmouth Rail Campaign in March 2014 kick-started local interest in the possibility of having the line re-opened.

Thanks to the enthusiasm and unrelenting campaigning of this group, the Scottish Government were finally persuaded that the re-introduction of passenger train services to Levenmouth would be of great benefit to the community; and, in August 2019, the announcement was made that the line was to re-open.

The news was enthusiastically received by everyone who had campaigned for the re-opening over the preceding years; and, of course, by the residents of the Levenmouth area. If all goes to plan, the line from Thornton to Leven will re-open in 2023, with new stations built at Leven and CameronBridge.

For further detailed information, please visit the LMRC website at: levenmouth.co.uk

It had been the Fife Heritage Railway Group's intention to take over part of the line as a tourist attraction. Whilst it will no longer be possible for this group to realise their ambition of running steam trains up and down the line, they are still very much alive; and, during the summer months, they will continue to operate steam and diesel services within the confines of the former Kirkland sidings, on the west side of Leven. They are well worth a visit, and Kirkland Yard can be accessed by following the signposts from the roundabout at the junction of Glenlyon Road and Leven Vale.

There has also been much debate regarding the re-introduction of a passenger train service to St Andrews. Starlink, an action group set up to press for the re-introduction of rail services to the University town, have been campaigning for several years, and have received considerable support and media coverage. The main difficulty with this ambitious project, however, is the fact that the track has long since been removed between St Andrews and the main line and this would have to be re-laid at considerable expense.

If the railway to St Andrews is ever re-opened, the possibility exists that it would not follow it's original 1852 course via Guardbridge to Leuchars, but would instead be built as a rail link between St Andrews and Cupar, where a junction with the main line could be made. This possibility may at first glance appear a little over ambitious; but no more so than the proposals put forward by a certain group of St Andrews gentlemen almost a century and a half earlier!

The Fife Heritage Railway, which falls under the auspices of the Kingdom of Fife Railway Preservation Society, operate steam trains over a section of re-laid track on the site of Kirkland sidings during the summer months.

For further information please visit their website at:

www.fifeheritagerailway.co.uk

ACKNOWLEDGEMENTS

There are many people who have been a great help in the production of this book.

In particular my thanks go to Mr Bruce Ellis of Ramsbottom in Lancashire; to John Doig and The Scottish Fisheries Museum in Anstruther; to the Archive Committee of the Kingdom of Fife Railway Preservation Society and to the staff of the Public Libraries at Cupar, Methil, Kirkcaldy and Anstruther.

I would also like to thank Mrs Joan Kingscott of Churchdown in Gloucestershire for access to her book collection, from which I have gained much useful information.

SOURCES AND BIBLIOGRAPHY

The information used in the writing of this book has been gathered mainly by spending many hours perusing through old newspapers in the Public Libraries in Cupar, Kirkcaldy, Methil and Anstruther. Other valuable information was gained by visiting the Scottish Records Office in Charlotte Square, Edinburgh.

The newspapers that provided so much pleasure during my research were The Fifeshire Journal, The Fifeshire Advertiser, The East of Fife Record, The East Fife Observer, The East Fife Mail, The Pittenweem Register and The Dundee Courier.

I have also gained much useful information about the fishing industry in the East Neuk of Fife from "The Lammas Drave and the Winter 'Herrin" by Peter Smith, published by John Donald in 1985.

Other books that proved to be invaluable during many hours of painstaking research were the "Handy Book of the Fife Coast" by Henry Farnie; "Fife: Pictorial and Historical" by A. H. Millar; "Random Reflections of a Roving Railwayman" by J. M. Bennett; the book simply entitled "Anstruther" by George Gourlay; "Forgotten Railways of Scotland" by John Thomas; "The Railways of Fife" by William Scott Bruce; "East Fife Railway Album" by Richard Batchelor; and "Scottish Freight Only Lines" by Mike Macdonald.

Suggested Further Reading

If you enjoyed this book, you might also enjoy the following publications by **Wast-By Books**, *all of which are available in both paperback and Kindle eBook format from Amazon.co.uk:*

Dyker Lad

Recollections of Life in an East Neuk of Fife Fishing Village before, during and after the Second World War

ISBN: 9781981019137

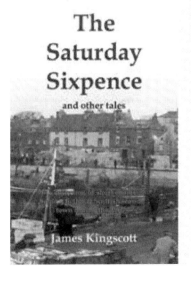

The Saturday Sixpence

a collection of short stories set in a fictional Scottish seaside town during the 1960's

ISBN: 9798556376090

Other Publications available from Wast-By Books:

On That Windswept Plain: The First One Hundred years of East Fife Football Club

(James K. Corstorphine, 2003)

ISBN: 9781976888618

Our Boys and the Wise Men: The Origins of Dundee Football Club

(James K. Corstorphine, 2020)

ISBN: 9798643521549

The Earliest Fife Football Clubs: Fife Football in the Late Nineteenth Century

(James K. Corstorphine, 2018)

ISBN 9781980249580

A Selection of Poems by 'Poetry Peter' Smith, the Fisherman Poet of Cellardyke

(Compiled by James K. Corstorphine, 2000)

ISBN 9798644727827

All of the above titles are available in both Paperback and Kindle eBook formats from: amazon.co.uk

Just one more thing before you go . . .

Your opinion would be very much appreciated!

I would be most grateful if you could find a few minutes to rate this book on Amazon.

I will take the time to read any comments made, and any suggestions as to how I can improve the publication will be taken on board.

Thank you!

James K. Corstorphine

Printed in Great Britain
by Amazon

59744229R00071